She Doesn't Look Deaf

Corinne Cheatham

Metier Books

ISBN: 978-1-32550-366-4 PB
1-59526-036-6 HC

Printed in the United States of America by Llumina Press

Dedication

This book is dedicated to my beautiful and precious daughter, Aaliyah, who brings so much joy to my life and to my wonderful husband, André, for his patience and understanding on those many evenings I spent on the book. God has truly blessed me.

Heavenly Perfection

A deaf child is born to hearing parents.
At first there is sadness, then acceptance.

There is thanks to God for our beautiful and healthy daughter.
Our home is full of love and joy.

Sign language fills the air.
Signal lights flash throughout our home.

Society labels deafness as a disability.
Businesses look at deafness as a financial burden.

As we grow wiser, our daughter grows older.
She is surrounded by our love.

Our daughter conquers society with great success.
Our hearts are full of pride.

The day comes for us to move to our new home.
At first there is sadness, then acceptance.

As the pearly gates slowly open, God is waiting.
He greets us by signing "Welcome, my children."

To our surprise, all of heaven's angels are signing.
No one is talking.

As we begin to talk, no words are spoken.
Instead, we find ourselves signing flawlessly.

God explains, "In heaven we are all deaf"
One night while visiting my daughter, I share this great news.

"Wake up my beautiful daughter, I have something to tell you."
Be proud of yourself and of being deaf because you are heav-
enly perfection.

By Corinne Cheatham

Chapter 1

Aaliyah's Early Entrance into the World

Everyone experiences life-changing events whether they are the result of the choices we make or they are thrown at us unexpectedly. No matter which is the case we learn from our choices and grow emotionally and intellectually as individuals. Without choices, we can't experience change and without change life becomes stagnant. I know that dealing with change takes strength and sometimes it's just easier to live comfortably without the added stressors life brings. I used to be a person who liked being comfortable but over the years I have grown to a person who likes change; perhaps change is my comfort zone. I can honestly say that I am proud of the choices I have made and where those choices have led me. I believe that God has a map for all of us, which leads us to our ultimate destination in life. My map led me to my husband, Andre' and daughter, Aaliyah. This is my story or road map to the ever-changing, emotional and rewarding journey of motherhood while raising a deaf child in the 21st century.

In 1994, I was living in Louisiana as a result of my military career in the Army Nurse Corp. During my four years on active duty I was stationed in Texas, San Francisco, Hawaii and then Ft. Polk, Louisiana (a place most soldiers would like to avoid). Prior to being honorably discharged in April, my boss had asked me to think about staying in the military. I replied sarcastically that if I could get a guarantee that I would not be sent overseas to any conflict and not have to participate in the Physical Fitness program I would stay in. My boss and I chuckled because we both knew that I was not a "lifer" and staying in the Army was not an option for me. However, I did offer to continue to work in the hospital as a civilian because I enjoyed the work and the people. I didn't mind living in the South and liked being in the same time zone as my family. I was even becoming accustomed to the fact that my name was no longer Corinne but "Honey."

In the winter, my husband and I found out that I was pregnant and we were very excited! I bought a pregnancy calendar that explained how a baby develops as the trimesters progressed and all my doctor's appointments were penciled in. I felt as if I was back in college preparing for a big final exam minus the caffeine fix and maintaining a healthy body was the key to passing the exam.

Seven months had gone by and I felt really good. I never experienced morning sickness and during all of my prenatal visits, the doctor assured me that Aaliyah was fine and gave me a clean bill of health. In May 1995, I just finished working a stretch of nights and looked forward to catching up on my sleep during my days off. On May 21st at 4:00 a.m., I began to have intense stomach cramps-apparently contractions, a pain I had never experienced before. My husband woke up concerned and asked me what was wrong. In between breaths of pain, I told him that I was just having some cramping and would be fine but after about 20 minutes of what seemed like one continuous cramp I was not fine. My husband insisted that we go to the hospital and during the entire 40-minute drive I had a death grip on his hand.

After we arrived at the hospital around 5:00 a.m., we rushed to the Labor and Delivery Unit. The doctor examined me and told me that I had started to dilate. He said that he would need to give me medication to slow down the contractions because he didn't want me to deliver since it was seven weeks before my due date. Almost four hours later, I was still dilating and the contractions were still coming. It was official, I was going to have our baby and I was in pain. For all of you "I'm going to have my baby without medication" moms, I'm proud to inform you that I begged for drugs. When I got that shot, my husband waited outside the room near the nurses' station. He said that I screamed so loud that I probably woke up everyone in the hospital. Well, I was experiencing excruciating pain and I wanted to make sure that everyone knew it.

Once the medication took effect, I was able to rest and concentrate on picking out some names. We hadn't picked out any names yet because we thought we had plenty of time. I didn't want to have our baby discharged from the hospital with the name Baby girl or boy, the generic name given to babies whose parents couldn't think of a name. Picking out a name is so important and can really have an impact on a child's social status growing up. I didn't want our child teased for his or her name. As a nurse, I have come across many odd names in my career; however, nothing takes the cake like Baby Meconium. For all of you non health care professionals, meconium is a baby's first "poop". Apparently, the mother heard the term being used by the nurses and thought it sounded pretty. What about it sounds pretty I have no idea and at that moment, I received confirmation that stupid people do live among us.

I wanted to pick out a name that would be beautiful and loved by our child. For whatever the reason, it seemed easier focusing on girl names rather than boy names. Perhaps, subconsciously we knew we were having a girl since all of the ultrasounds showed a baby with legs crossed. We finally decided on the name Aaliyah because it was beautiful and uncommon. We had not heard the name except for a popular singer at the time. If we did have a boy, he would be out of luck for a few days and would have to be called Baby Boy Cheatham.

After five ½ hours in the hospital, the doctor ruptured my water bag and discovered that Aaliyah's legs were facing toward the birth canal. As a result of her positioning and prematurity, I was told that I would need to have a cesarean section. Although I had the medical background to understand the situation, I was still really scared. How could this happen? At all of my doctor's appointments, I was told that we were fine. I stopped drinking products with caffeine and did all the things I could do to make sure that Aaliyah was growing in a healthy environment. Nevertheless, it was finally time for me to be wheeled to the operating room. As I lay there awake on the operating table supposedly numb from the waist down, I could feel the doctor pulling apart my abdomen where the incision was made. Shocked at the thought that I still had feeling and pain, I quickly told the doctor who then gave me general anesthesia.

Seven weeks before Aaliyah's due date, at 11:47 a.m., on May 21st, my husband and I were blessed with a beautiful but wrinkled (a common look for premature babies) daughter. She weighed 4 pounds and 2 ounces and was 17 inches long making her small enough to fit into the palm of my husband's hand. Immediately after her birth the doctor and nurses needed to stabilize Aaliyah so she could be transported to a Neonatal Intensive Care Unit (NICU), which was located in a different hospital two hours away. She was given blow-by oxygen because she was having some trouble breathing on her own. After several attempts of placing an IV so she could get fluids and antibiotics, one was started in her umbilical cord vein. Shortly after being stabilized and just before the transfer, a nurse wheeled Aaliyah in her transport incubator next to the gurney that I was on so I could see her for a brief moment. To my disappointment, all I saw was a tiny blur since I had forgotten my glasses in the car.

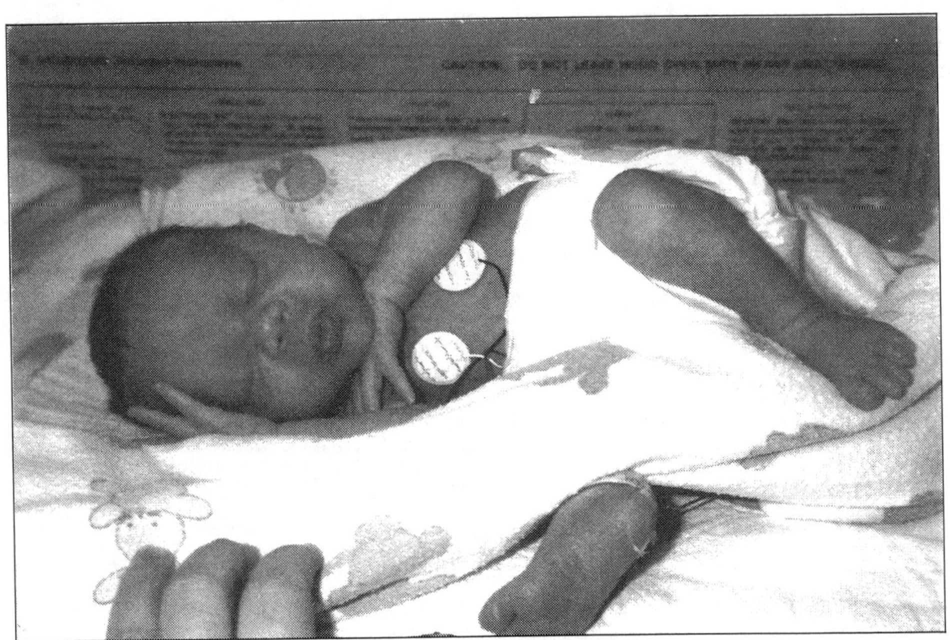

Aaliyah in the NICU after her birth.

I remained in the hospital for three lonely days without my daughter. This was especially hard to deal with as I watched grandparents, family members, and friends come to visit the other babies. I really missed my family although my husband was a great support. I can honestly say that nothing about the hospital stay was pleasant and I was bored out of my mind. I suffered in silence as I listened to the other women talk about their babies as they held them. It was not until five days after Aaliyah's birth that I was able to make the commute with my husband to see our precious baby.

My first clear look at Aaliyah was filled with amazement. Her tiny body was in an incubator surrounded by blankets molded to fit around her body so she would not slip down on the mattress as it was slightly tilted. There was a tube in her nose, which provided her with food since she was too little and weak to feed from a bottle. The room was filled with beeping heart monitors, buzzing incubators, and other equipment needed to take care of premature babies. It was then that I was finally able to make sure that she was OK. I was so relieved to see that she had 10 fingers and toes and overall was doing pretty well for being born seven weeks early. I felt truly blessed because God had given me a wonderful husband and a beautiful and healthy baby. I couldn't ask for anything more.

As the days became weeks, Aaliyah grew stronger and stronger. She fed from a bottle and gained weight, all signs that meant she would be coming home soon. The last week in the hospital, she was able to maintain a body temperature that allowed her to come out of the incubator and stay in a regular bassinet. It was while she was in the regular bassinet that she had her hearing screened.

Louisiana at the time screened the hearing in all high-risk infants and Aaliyah met one of the criteria by being born premature. In 1995, only two states, Hawaii and Rhode Island, had legislative mandates that required all babies born in that state have their hearing screened. As of 2005, Louisiana is one of 38 states which have enacted Newborn Hearing Screening Legislation and screens all babies and not just high risk infants. Washington, the state we currently live in, has not passed legislation on newborn hearing screenings and in 2004, 85.5% of newborns had their hearing screened. According to the National Center on Birth Defects and Developmental Disabilities the cost of a hearing screening is about $30.00 per child and takes about nine minutes to do. To view the specific nature of the legislation passed in the states mentioned above, go to www.infanthearing.org/legislative/index.html.

Proud dad showing off Aaliyah.

Aaliyah and mom the night before going home from the hospital.

The night before Aaliyah was discharged home, I spent the night in the hospital with her because it was hospital policy for mothers to "room-in" with their baby so that they get initiated into the routine of motherhood. I was so excited and nervous about being a mother. Would I be a good mother? Would I know what to do when it needed to be done? Although I had worked in a nursery feeding newborn babies, bathing them, and changing their diapers, this was my baby and it was different.

On June 11th, 1995, Aaliyah was discharged from the hospital. Hooray! No more three-hour commutes, wearing hospital gowns and scrubbing our hands for one minute every time we entered the NICU. We bundled her up, packed her clothes, and got the car seat ready. The nurse gave us our discharge paperwork, which reminded us to schedule an appointment with an audiologist since Aaliyah failed the hearing screenings. We were so excited to leave the hospital and anxious to get home that making appointments was the furthest thing from my mind.

Once at home we got Aaliyah settled in her room, which was decorated with Lion King characters on the wall, an animal mobile over her crib, and animal print bedding. A cassette player was positioned near the head of the crib, ready to play jazzy lullaby songs. A few days later, I scheduled a hearing test on June 29th when she would be a little over one month old. I was sure that everything would be just fine because I really thought that as her neurological system matured her hearing would be fine and as a nurse I knew that sometimes screenings are not absolute.

Before Aaliyah's scheduled hearing test, we did our own tests at home. One day my husband vacuumed her room to see if she would respond to the noise but she didn't. She was sound asleep and didn't make any type of movement that indicated that she heard the vacuum cleaner. Another test we performed involved banging pots and pans together while she was asleep or playing in the crib. This had similar results as the previous test with one exception; not only were we startled by the noise but we ended up with major headaches as well.

Except for the occasional testing we did at home, we really didn't focus on Aaliyah's hearing loss because she was happy and healthy. We would talk to her in that cute baby talk that everyone does and I would sing to her while I rocked her to sleep. She responded with smiles and coos just as all babies' do to meaningful and loving interactions with parents. She was perfect to us.

Chapter 2

The Road to Diagnosis

The day of Aaliyah's first official hearing test finally came and I was really nervous. I knew that this test would be more accurate than the screening that was done in the hospital so I prayed for normal results. This official hearing test was called an Auditory Brain Stem Response (ABR). An ABR is a test that measures the hearing nerve and the brain's response to sound. It is commonly done on infants or small children because it doesn't require that they tell or show the sounds they heard. As I sat in the chair holding Aaliyah, the audiologist prepared her for the ABR by taping small surface disks to her forehead and behind each of her ears. Small foam-tipped earphones were placed in both of her ears. After the testing equipment was turned on, the machine made clicking sounds that went through the earphones and recorded Aaliyah's response on a tracing that would let the audiologist know what degree of hearing loss she had. These results were then documented on a graph called an audiogram, which in essence is a picture of one's hearing. The test took about 30-45 minutes and I was told that according to the manufacturers of the equipment the test is greater than 98% accurate and results are very reliable.

After the test was finished, the audiologist told me that Aaliyah didn't pass and that she had a severe hearing loss, with the left ear worse than the right. She didn't respond to sounds at 95 decibels (dB) in either ear, which was the loudest the equipment would go. I was shocked to learn that she had the most severe hearing loss. Why did this happen to my baby? I was so overwhelmed with all of this information that I had experienced brief moments of disbelief, denial and anger. However, I was not going to accept the fact that she had such a severe hearing loss until she had a few more ABRs. This was my way of coping because I thought that as long as there were hearing tests, I could continue to hope that the results would get better.

When Aaliyah was around four months old, I went back to working the night shift. André was with her at night and I was with her during the day, which gave me the flexibility to schedule her necessary appointments. While at work, I utilized the hospital's medical library and took every opportunity I could to read literature on hearing loss. Working in the hospital gave me the opportunity to become familiar with many of the people involved with Aaliyah's medical care. I couldn't have arranged our lives any better given our situation. Once you have a child with or without special needs, your day revolves around them. I realize that others may not be as fortunate when it comes to family and work but remember, family should come first and once this is made a priority, everything else will fall into place.

When Aaliyah had her second ABR, I prayed that the results would show a mild hearing loss, however, reality dictated otherwise and the results remained unchanged from the first test. ABR appointments became an integral part of our lives along with routine visits to the pediatrician and other specialists. The medical support we received from the military was awesome and the doctors were very thorough in making sure that there were no other medical conditions accompanying her hearing loss.

In October of 1995, we traveled to San Antonio, TX to have her evaluated by specialists at Brooke Army Medical Center. The first specialist we saw was an Ear, Nose, and Throat (ENT) doctor, who examined Aaliyah to make sure that structurally there was nothing wrong with her ears. He also gave us some basic information on Cochlear Implants and told us that if we wanted to get this done, Aaliyah would need to be two years old. After his visit, he referred us to the next specialist.

The second specialist was a cardiologist or heart doctor, who examined Aaliyah to make sure she didn't have a syndrome called Jervell and Lange-Nielsen Syndrome, which is characterized by congenital sensorineural deafness and a change in the heartbeat's rhythm. Children who are affected with this are prone to fainting spells and sudden death due to fatal ventricular arrhythmias. Aaliyah had an EKG done to make sure that she had normal heart rhythms and a chest x-ray to make sure that her heart was a normal size. Everything was fine.

The third specialist we saw was an ophthalmologist or eye doctor, who made sure that Aaliyah did not have any visual dysfunctions. He had to rule out the possibility of Aaliyah having Usher Syndrome, which is a genetic condition characterized by sensorineural hearing loss and a disease of the retina called Retinitis Pigmentosa. After her eyes were dilated, the Ophthalmologist examined them with a light through an otoscope. He told us that by looking at the nerves in the back of Aaliyah's eyes he could tell if she had gone through any trauma that may have caused her hearing loss. The exam went well.

The last doctor we saw was a genetic specialist whose job was to see if Aaliyah had inherited her hearing loss. He took a brief history and then did an exam which involved measuring the space between her eyes, the space between her eyes and ears and looked at her nail beds. He concluded that her hearing loss was probably an isolated congenital deafness and recommended that we get a renal ultrasound done to look for anything abnormal with her kidneys. Some conditions involving the kidneys may have hearing loss associated with it. Two syndromes characterized by neurosensory hearing loss and kidney failure include Alport Syndrome and Branchio-oto-Renal Syndrome.

After all the appointments were done, Aaliyah was given a clean bill of health. She had no other medical conditions and her hearing loss was diagnosed as sensorineural and congenital which meant that the hearing loss was present when she was born and they did not know the cause. There are three types of hearing loss: conductive, sensorineural, and mixed.

Conductive hearing loss may present itself when something interferes with sound waves traveling through the outer and middle parts of the ear. One type of interference may be caused by complete blockage in the outer ear by wax. Infection in the middle ear may be another type of interference. Lastly, damage to the tiny bones in the middle ear may cause interference with sound waves.

Sensorineural hearing loss results from a problem in the inner ear or in the hearing nerve. This type of hearing loss is more likely to be permanent. One cause of sensorineural hearing loss may be diseases such as meningitis and rubella. Tumors can cause sensorineural hearing loss. Abnormal development of the inner part of the ear and other genetic conditions may cause this type of hearing loss. Lastly, physical injury to the inner ear can cause sensorineural hearing loss.

Mixed hearing loss is a combination of sensorineural hearing loss and conductive hearing loss. After the diagnosis, the audiologist told us that one in every 1,000 babies born has a hearing loss, in more than 50% of these cases the cause of the hearing loss is unknown and 90% of these babies have hearing parents. Today, the number of babies born with a hearing loss is three in 1,000. What this statistic indicates is not that there are more children born today with a hearing loss but that there are more babies being identified with a hearing loss because more states have mandatory hearing screenings.

According to the Early Hearing Detection and Intervention Information and Resource Center (EHDI) "Every day, 33 babies (or 12,000 each year) are born in the United States with permanent hearing loss. With three of every 1,000 newborns having a hearing loss, it is the most frequently occurring birth defect." Considering the statistics, I was amazed that at the time of Aaliyah's birth I had been a pediatric nurse for five years and had not met any hearing-impaired children. In fact, up to that point, I had not met any hearing-impaired adults in my life. What was God's plan for my husband and I in blessing us with such a special child?

In a poem from the summer 1996 edition of The Endeavor, a publication from the American Society for Deaf Children, I was reminded of what a privilege it is from God to be a parent. Also, special consideration goes into picking parents of children with special needs. After reading this poem I was honored that God believed that my husband and I were qualified to be Aaliyah's parents. The author of this poem is unknown.

Heaven's Special Child

A meeting was held quite far from earth,
"It's time again for another birth."

Said the Angels of the Lord above,
"This special child will need much love."

His progress may seem very slow,
Accomplishments he may not show.

And he'll require much extra care,
From all the folks he meets down there.

He may not laugh or run or play,
His thought may seem quite far away.

In many ways he won't adapt,
And he'll be known as "handicapped".

So let's be careful where he's sent,
We want his life to be content.

Please Lord, Find the parents who,
Will do this special job for you.

They will not realize right away,
The leading role they're asked to play.

But with this child sent from above,
Comes stronger faith and richer love.

And soon they'll know the privilege given,
In caring for this gift from Heaven.

This precious child, so meek and mild,
Is "Heaven's Very Special Child."

Author Unknown

Prior to Aaliyah's third hearing test and through the fog of on and off denial, I began to search for the cause of her hearing loss. I expected answers after the appointments with the specialists. Instead I was told, your child is healthy and we don't know why she has a hearing loss. My experience as a nurse has taught me that parents look for answers when they go to a health professional. They want to know why their child is sick and what caused it to happen. I was no different and deep down I think we, as parents want to know if we are responsible for our child's illness or disability because it's human nature to seek blame for that which is not "perfect."

In November of 1995, Aaliyah had her third hearing test when she was six months old. My hope of better test results evaporated after the audiologist told me that the results were consistent with the first two tests. I finally had to accept her severe to profound hearing loss. It didn't matter how many more hearing tests were going to be done because my baby was not going to hear. I felt sad because I was worried about how hard growing up would be for her without hearing. Of course this fear stemmed from my lack of knowledge about the Deaf culture and how deaf people live. As a nurse who has seen many families deal with more intense obstacles in life, I knew that

I could handle Aaliyah's deafness and I was excited to learn all I could related to having a deaf child especially how to communicate with her.

Aaliyah's hearing loss was classified as severe to profound. Classifications are based on their severity and the degree of loss is determined by measuring the hearing threshold, which is measured in decibels (dB). The hearing threshold is the softest sound heard and when sound is made louder so that it is barely heard. This represents the degree of hearing loss. There are four degrees of hearing loss: mild, moderate, severe and profound.

Children with mild hearing loss can hear sounds of 26 - 45dB or louder. Sounds that fall within this range include clocks ticking, leaves rustling and people whispering. Normal hearing is a response to sound up to 25 dB.

Children with moderate hearing loss can hear sounds louder than 46 -65 dB while those with severe losses can hear sound of 66-85 dB or louder. Examples of sounds that fall within this range are trains moving and vacuum cleaners operating. This is the level when the term "deaf" is used.

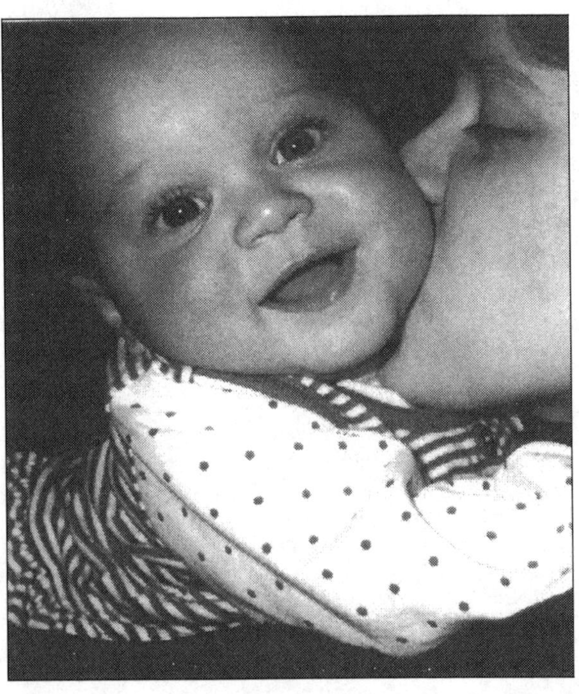

Aaliyah getting a big hug and kiss from mom Feb 1996

Real life doll, Aaliyah at 8 months old with her porcelain friend at Grandma and Grandpa's house

Profound hearing loss involves hearing loud sounds of 85 dB or more, but children may be more aware of vibrations than sound. Some examples of sounds heard in this category include rock concerts, jackhammers, motorcycles, ambulance or fire sirens and jet engine at takeoff. With this level of hearing loss, hearing aids may or may not help and cochlear implants are often an option.

Children with a hearing loss that crosses two levels of severity are given the diagnosis of both. For example, Aaliyah's degree of hearing loss was severe-profound. We used this term for months until I realized that it was a mouthful to say and people really didn't grasp what the term meant. However, when I told people that she was "Deaf" then they understood that this meant that she could not hear.

Following the third test, the audiologist recommended that Aaliyah be fitted with behind the ear hearing aids for both ears. He told us that he would select the aids that would provide her with the most amplification for her hearing loss. The first step to getting fitted was that we would need to bring her in for another visit to have molds of her ear canal made. At this visit, the audiologist made a temporary mold by mixing water with a powder to get a caulk like consistency. After he injected this substance into the ear opening we waited about 5-10 minutes for the mold to harden. At times this was difficult because I had to keep her head from moving around. Once the mold hardened it was sent out to a company that would make the final mold from a soft plastic. The soft plastic mold sat in the ear opening attached to the body of the hearing aids (which housed the amplifier, battery and microphone).

The Army covered all the costs related to the equipment needed for Aaliyah's hearing loss, which was truly a financial relief to us. After a week or so, we finally got the hearing aids that cost $1,700 a piece and the molds were around $40.00 per set. I was so excited to see how much she would be able to hear with them but I was surprised to see how big the hearing aids were. They were as long as her ears and as wide as an adult's index finger. The hearing aids were the same color as her skin so from a distance they were less noticeable, however up close they were huge and therefore obvious. I asked about the hearing aids that were small enough to fit in the ear canal, but I was told that those were not powerful enough for her hearing loss.

According to the audiologist, Aaliyah had the Cadillac model of hearing aids because they were the best and most powerful on the market at the time. Although we could not be certain of the benefit she would get from the hearing aids, the goals in wearing them were two-fold. The first goal was to amplify sounds to stimulate her hearing nerve, which in turn would help it get stronger and stronger. The second goal was to retrain her hearing system within the brain so that she would be more successful with interpreting the sounds she heard.

Hearing aids were a struggle at this age because developmentally, Aaliyah began to grab onto things and was fascinated with her hands, toes, and finding her ears. She constantly pulled on her aids causing a lot of feedback (whistling). Also, at this age babies start to develop more head control by moving their head from side to side or trying to lift their head up. When Aaliyah did this the ear molds shifted causing feedback because they were not fitted tightly. Having the volume set to high or removing and inserting the hearing aids while they were turned on was another cause of feedback. The audiologist said that Aaliyah could not hear the whistle but it was a sound my husband and I heard frequently. Eventually, we dealt with the whistling by adjusting the hearing aids when we heard it. The sound eventually became as common as the phone ringing or the birds chirping and when the feedback became constant that indicated it was time to get new ear molds made. We had to get new ear molds made about every four months due to changes within Aaliyah's ear canal as she grew.

Four weeks had gone by since Aaliyah got her hearing aids and it was time for her first ABR with hearing aids on. I had been watching her closely to see if she would respond to sounds by either being startled or turning her head. I didn't see any of these responses but I knew that retraining her brain to hear with the aids would be a long process. I began to have hope again because I thought that each ABR result would show improvement as she wore her aids longer and longer. During the ABR, Aaliyah's left ear was tested with the hearing aid but the right hearing aid was producing a lot of feedback so it wasn't tested. The results noted a possible startle to the audiologist's voice at 80-85 dB. This was consistent with the findings of the other tests.

Although, I had suspicions that the results would not be dramatic, I was still praying for more than what I saw. At this point, Aaliyah's hearing continued to be within the severe to profound range with or without hearing aids. I began to dislike going to these appointments because it was such an emotional roller coaster. I came feeling hopeful and left feeling angry. Was this all a waste of time? How much longer was this necessary? I wanted to make sure that I was doing everything I could for Aaliyah and felt that somehow searching for the cause of her hearing loss was going to help in some way. I gathered all of her medical records and reviewed the information hoping to find something in writing why Aaliyah was deaf. Since Aaliyah was in the NICU for three weeks, I often wondered if this had some effect on her hearing loss because while researching literature related to neonates and noise exposure, I came across the following information.

According to the American Academy of Pediatrics, Committee on Environmental Health, it is recommended that a maximum safe noise level of

45 dB in the NICU be maintained. However, research shows that persistent exposure to the following sounds can cause hearing loss. First, closing the metal cabinet doors under the incubator when the nurses or we would get formula, diapers, or Aaliyah's tee shirts produced sounds up to 90 dB the equivalent of a pneumatic drill. Second, by closing the solid plastic portholes in the incubator without opening the whole top of the incubator produced sounds up to 100dB the equivalent of a lawn mower. Third, the act of dropping the head of the mattress in the incubator produced sounds up to 120 dB the equivalent of a car stereo system. Although these acts were done to provide quality care for Aaliyah in effect may have exposed her sensitive ears and immature nervous system to the noise level of a rock concert. Imagine being at a rock concert 24/7 for almost three weeks. Along with this information, I primarily focused on the medications she received that had documented hearing loss as a side effect. I took my information to a local attorney, pursuing a medical malpractice claim. The attorney I consulted with stated that it would be very difficult to maintain a malpractice claim for a number of reasons.

The first reason was that there were an extreme number of risks surrounding the birth of a premature infant. The second reason was that in the event that the doctor could justify his administration of the medications together with the dosage amount so as to prevent another risk or life threatening event, then this could not be maintained as malpractice.

The last reason given was that because of his specialty, another Neonatologist in the community would need to be consulted and would have to basically testify that the doctor was acting beyond his specialty and this was not a reasonable action for him to take within his specialty. There was only one other Neonatologist in the community and he was about two hours away. The attorney doubted that he would be willing to testify. I was not happy with this information and was encouraged by the attorney to get a second opinion, which I did and it was the same as the first opinion.

In July of 1996, I consulted with a third attorney, who stated that under Louisiana law, a person has one year from the date that he or she knew or was on notice, of the possibility of medical malpractice within which to bring a claim, or the statute of limitation will forever bar bringing a suit. Because there was some uncertainty as to whether or not the statute had in fact run out, I was encouraged to file on Aaliyah's behalf a claim with the Louisiana Patient's Compensation Fund Oversight Board. I did write a letter to the Board but the reply I got stated that I would need to be more specific in regards to the health care provider as well as the date of the alleged malpractice.

Well, no matter how hard I tried to focus on enjoying life with my daughter regardless of the fact she was deaf, I could not squash my curiosity related to "why" she was deaf. Periodically, I had to travel down that road. A couple years after Aaliyah birth, I began to wonder if genetics played any part in her deafness. My husband knew of no one in his family who was deaf so I thought maybe this came from my side of the family. However, this was not an easy question to answer because I was adopted. I hired a private investigator hoping to find an answer and eventually did find by biological mother. Unfortunately, our meeting only spawned more questions and uncertainty even though at the time she said that there was no one in the family who was deaf.

Once again, just before Aaliyah turned five years old, I had been cleaning the house and heard a commercial for an attorney's office that dealt with medical malpractice.

Chapter 3

To Sign or Not to Sign

Due to Aaliyah's special needs, we were required to enroll in the Army's Exceptional Family Members Program (EFMP). The purpose of this program was to match her needs to the available special education and medical services within the area. It was through EFMP we were referred to the Louisiana's Early Intervention Program, which was called the Sound Start Program. Early Intervention services help families who have children with disabilities from birth to three. These services are federally mandated under Part C of the Individuals with Disabilities Education Act, which is our nation's special education law that guides how states and school districts provide special education and related services to students with disabilities. Every state's Early Intervention Program offers a variety of services and for Deaf and Hard of Hearing Children these services may provide assistance with the following: assistive technology such as signalers for the door and telephone, TTY's, hearing devices and fitting them, testing a child's hearing, teaching a family how to communicate with a deaf child through counseling and home visits, classes on sign language and speech therapy.

I can't stress enough the importance for families to get connected with the Early Intervention Program in their state. The first five years of a child's life are very important for brain development so if you have not been plugged into your state's Program put this book down and call now. The state of Washington's Early Intervention Program is called Infant Toddler Early Intervention Program (ITEIP) and their number is 360-725-3516. For information on Early Intervention Programs in other states contact The National Early Childhood Technical Assistance Center at 1-919-962-2001 or go to their website at www.nectac.org . I would also recommend that a parent contact the school district in which they live in, their child's doctor office, or the Department of Health to get a contact number for a program near them.

The Sound Start Program was an important building block in our journey to successfully communicate with Aaliyah. We were introduced to a beginning sign language class that was held at the local elementary school and an Early Intervention Specialist, who came to our home twice a week. At these home visits we were taught how to communicate with Aaliyah using sign language and play. The Early Intervention Specialist also provided us with resources related to the Deaf culture including a meeting with a deaf woman. I was really nervous about this meeting because I had never met a deaf person and I was worried about communicating with her. This woman grew up orally which meant that she did not use sign language but read lips very well. Nonetheless, I was pleasantly surprised that we were able to communicate without too much difficulty. We had talked for hours about how she grew up, what types of teaching methods her family used and what an impact her mother had on her. She stressed that her success in life was because her mother worked very hard with her every day on reading, writing, and speaking.

After spending some time at our home we drove to her place so she could show me how the deaf communicate via a phone, called a TTY. A TTY is a teletypewriter that has a typewriter and a display associated with a telephone that allows hearing or speech impaired persons to communicate over the telephone line to another person that also has a TTY. She also showed me how her home was set up with signal lights so that when the doorbell rang or the telephone rang a series of lights would flash to alert her. The whole visit was very fascinating and I took away two important bits of information. One was that parents are very important in the success of their children and if you are not willing to put 110% into raising your children than don't have them. The other thing was that it was very hard to talk with a deaf person at night in the car.

As we continued to receive services through the Sound Start Program, I began to investigate the local educational system to see if it would be able to provide Aaliyah with the services required for deaf children three years of age and older? The answer was a definite NO. The school district didn't have any deaf and hard of hearing programs and the nearest school with such a program was almost three hours away.

If we stayed in the area long enough for Aaliyah to enroll in the school system, she would have been in a Pre-kindergarten/kindergarten classroom with hearing children, children with multiple disabilities, and one other hearing-impaired child. The teacher knew sign language but lacked the background in deaf education. This was not the educational environment I wanted for her. How could she learn at the same level as her hearing peers? She needed to learn the language in order to comprehend it while her hearing peers worked on comprehension because they had already learned the language. Also, if a hearing-impaired child is placed in a classroom with children who have multiple disabilities, there is a possibility that the hearing-impaired child will begin to mimic the behavior of the other children. Well, thank goodness she would not be entering the school system for a few years so we had time to work on this.

In our journey to make the best decisions for our family, the Sound Start program showed us a small piece of what raising a deaf child in the 21st century involved. One of the primary needs of children is to have their needs met through communicating with those in their environment. If these needs are not met on a consistent basis then they become frustrated and develop behavioral problems. In order to avoid this, we continued to receive information on the different ways to communicate with Aaliyah through literature and home visits with the Early Intervention Specialist.

There are a number of ways to communicate with a deaf child. The communication approaches to choose from include: oral, sign language, total communication, and cued speech. There is never a wrong decision when it comes to communicating with a deaf child, however I consider the lack of communication a form of neglect. Our deaf children need to be in families that provide as much communication as possible so that they are able to share their dreams as well as their fears. Aaliyah did have some classmates that would only receive communication at school because the parents did nothing at home and I learned that these children often had behavioral issues at school. Well, I wonder why?

Children raised with an oral philosophy do not use sign language. They depend on amplification, lip reading, and speech skills to communicate. It is thought that since this is a hearing world, it is best to learn to communicate the way hearing people do. I thought it was interesting that the few deaf individuals I met who grew up this way ended up learning sign language. When examining this approach online, I came across a bulletin board in which a deaf person expressed her perspective on sign language. She wrote "My parents sent me to regular school, I was mainstreamed. I never learned sign, I had to learn to lip-read and speak. I am grateful for the speaking part, it helps out a lot now, but I will forever be disappointed that I did not learn to sign, because now I want to learn it and it's hard as an adult! My parents made the choice for me, I was only five, I couldn't have a say yet. But now looking back, believe me I wish they would have taught me sign. I would not be such an outsider in the Deaf community had they taught it to me. I'm stuck as an outsider in the hearing world because I have to have help to understand regular conversation, and I'll be an outsider in the Deaf community because I don't know sign and didn't grow up in the Deaf culture. Please consider this when you're making your decisions for your children. They can always drop sign language since it's much harder to pick it up later in life."

Oralists believe that sign language will either distract deaf children from learning speech or interfere with the motivation to learn it. I came across some family members who thought we were wrong for communicating with sign language. They fed into the belief that sign language was an easy way out and would cause Aaliyah to be lazy in learning how to talk. I certainly agree with the Oralists' belief that learning speech is important but I disagree with the notion that sign language will some how impede the speech learning process. If a child's hearing loss is such where they have a lot of residual hearing than perhaps it would be best for that family to focus on speech. For the child with a severe to profound hearing loss like Aaliyah I don't think it is fair to force her to communicate this way.

A poem I came across in the fall 1995 edition of The Endeavor really helped me feel better about choosing sign language as our communication mode.

A day in the park, summer 1996

Thoughts of a Deaf Child

By Stephen J. Bellitz

My family knew that I was deaf
When I was only three

And since then, fifteen years ago
Have never signed to me.

I know when I'm around my house
I try and use my voice.

It makes them feel more comfortable
For me, I have no choice.

I try, communicate their way.
Uncomfortable for me.

My parents wouldn't learn to sign
Ashamed, or apathy?

I never cared about the sound of
radios and bands;

What hurts me is, I never heard
My parents signing hands.

When I began to learn sign language I thought that sign language was the same in all countries but I quickly learned that this was not true. Most countries have their own sign language system. American Sign Language (ASL), Signing Exact English (SEE), and Pidgin Signed English (PSE) are commonly used sign methods in the United States and the first two sign systems are considered complete languages.

ASL is the native language of the Deaf community. It is a visual and gestural language that doesn't incorporate spoken English. All signs in ASL are conceptually based and it has its own complex grammar, its own rules of construction, and its own way of communicating meaning. ASL cannot be used simultaneously with voiced English.

Interest in ASL continues to grow and many sign language classes are being offered in libraries, churches, community centers and colleges. It is now the fourth most used language in the United States. According to an article published in the fall 1998 issue of the ERIC Review, 28 states have passed legislation recognizing ASL as a foreign language. These states have permitted high schools and universities (including Brown, Georgetown, the Massachusetts Institute of Technology, Purdue, and the University of Washington) to accept ASL for academic or elective credit. In the past few years I have had more and more parents tell me that their children are being taught sign language in the grade schools. I think this is wonderful and hope that as a result of more children knowing sign language there will be a bigger pool of friends for Aaliyah to interact with.

Some parents I meet are very set on learning ASL because they feel that their child is deaf and to be a part of the Deaf community ASL is the sign system to use. Growing up, I was never a follower or a leader. Perhaps, you would say I was an individualist with a small circle of friends. I would associate with people because they were kind and respectful and not because they belonged to a certain group. I just don't understand the logic of a parent who wants to immerse themselves and their child in ASL for the sole purpose of fitting in with the Deaf community. Hello, if your child is deaf and has the ability to communicate well with others, I am sure that both the Deaf and hearing communities will accept him/her. My ultimate goal has been to provide Aaliyah with all means of communication necessary to build her self-esteem to such a level that she would feel comfortable communicating with all people whether they are deaf or hearing.

SEE is a sign language system that has borrowed a great deal of signs from ASL and follows English exactly. This system was first made available in 1972 and today it is used in every state and in other countries too. With SEE, words are signed in English word order. Voicing and signing can be done simultaneously because as each word is spoken it is signed or finger spelled. Signs have been created for word endings, prefixes and suffixes. For example, the word toys would be signed "toy + s" or the word swimming would be signed "swim + ing." The boy is reading a book would be signed "The boy is read + ing a book." In ASL this sentence would be signed, "Book boy read." SEE has been easier to learn than ASL for me and I have found that other hearing parents of Deaf children agree.

I chose to learn and continue to learn both sign systems. It has been easier to take ASL classes since these are more prevalent within the community while SEE classes are only offered through workshops put on by the SEE center twice a year or through classes offered by the Northwest School for the Hearing Impaired in Seattle. Each sign system plays an important part in providing Aaliyah with a strong language base. Children are conceptual learners and therefore ASL explains the concept of materials better while SEE is much more effective for teaching reading and writing. Also, it allows children to see each word spoken as it is signed. I knew an interpreter who knew both sign systems. She preferred to use SEE when she interpreted for the young school age children and ASL for students in middle school and beyond. Although the two sign systems are different the individual words have fairly similar signs.

Pidgin Signed English (PSE) is a combination of the two systems. This tends to be widely used among hearing persons who work with the deaf. Many teachers use PSE unless the school program specifically requires the teacher to use ASL or SEE.

Our family has used ASL in the past and now we use SEE because that is what is taught at Aaliyah's school, Northwest School for Hearing Impaired Children. However, no matter what sign system we use, we are always signing and for the most part speaking at the same time, which is a technique, used within Total Communication. I believe this method to be the most effective way to communicate with a Deaf child.

The following is a poem written by a deaf poet/writer Linwood Smith. It really describes the beauty as well as the importance of sign language in the life of a deaf person.

A Poem
The Way of A Hand

By Linwood Smith

There's beauty in the way a hand
Can carve a word on air,

There's beauty in the way a hand
Can give lift to a prayer.

There's beauty in the way a hand
Can trace a song in space,

There's beauty in the way a hand
Can light a deaf child's face.

Though, we can't hear the spoken word
Or leaves rustling in a tree,

We can hear the beauty
Of a word that we can see.

There's beauty in the way a hand
Can make the things you say

Seem soft as rain, hard as stone,
And clear and bright as day.

The spoken word can't do these things,
But words in signs can be

More vivid and more meaningful,
For they're something we can see.

There's beauty in a child's attempts
To spell his first word "CAT."

There's beauty in the way he learns
To sign his first word "HAT,"

There's beauty in the way a hand
Can move so gracefully

When someone signs "a stream of light,"
Or "waves crashing on the sea."

Close your hands and cross them,
Draw them to your heart,

The word you sign is "LOVE"
And that's where signs should start.

Though, we can't hear the tinkle,
tinkle, tinkle of a bell,

We can hear the tinkle, tinkle,
tinkle when it's spelled.

Though, we can't hear the music
In the shells along the sea,

We can hear the music
Of a signed word's melody.

And being deaf we cannot hear
The baby when it cries.

Or the sharp loud crack of lightning
Sizzling down from darkening skies.

But we can hear the "cry and crack"
In all their majesty,

When they're clearly on the hand
And before our eyes to see.

Along with Sign Language, Total Communication or communicating orally, Cued Speech is another method. R. Orin Cornet invented Cued Speech in 1966. This is a system of communicating with eight hand shapes in four possible positions to supplement the information visible on the lips. It is a speech-based method of communication aimed at taking the guesswork out of speech reading. Maryland, Minnesota and North Carolina are states with a large cued speech public school system.

Whichever method of communicating a family chooses, the ability to communicate clearly with our children is the most important task we as parents will face. Not only will clear communication help to develop an integrated family, it will also allow our children to develop strong and independent personalities. Our children will be able to read, write, and accomplish their goals as well as their hearing peers.

I came across some alarming information related to the reading comprehension level of deaf students who had graduated from high school. According to information provided in 1999 by the Shared Reading Project from Gallaudet University, the average reading comprehension level of deaf students graduating from high school is between the 3rd and 4th grade level. I have yet to come across any current literature that offers different statistical information. This is not acceptable and obviously is happening for two reasons. First, as parents, we are not providing a strong foundation in language to our children at an early age. Second, there is definitely something lacking with the educational and support services that our children get.

Chapter 4

Where Do We Go From Here?

We accepted the fact that Aaliyah was deaf and decided to use sign language as our means of communication. We had just begun to get our feet wet in the water of special education services when I was ready to dive in and learn more about all the services we could get for Aaliyah. In order to get these services, the early intervention program coordinator of the local school district and the parent infant specialist helped us develop an Individualized Family Services Plan, or IFSP.

The IFSP is a document that identifies a family's strengths and needs as they relate to a child's development. The IFSP also clearly states the goals toward which the family and the early intervention team will be working on. Young children depend on their families for all their care and if the children are to be helped, their families must be helped, too. To make sure that happens, the law says that people who work with families of children with disabilities must make an IFSP for the whole family. This is required for families of children from birth to age three.

While we were living in Louisiana, we had two IFSP meetings in our home. Aaliyah's IFSP was developed by the Early Intervention Coordinator of the local school district, the parent infant specialist, my husband and myself. The main goals of the IFSP focused on communicating with Aaliyah through sign language and developing her hearing and language skills. I understood the need to work on sign language since that would be our family's main way of communicating. However, since Aaliyah was deaf how would we develop her listening skills? I had many questions related to how we would meet this goal. Thank goodness the parent infant specialist provided us with information and activities that would help with this goal. She explained that although Aaliyah was deaf, she might have a small amount of hearing that she needed to learn to use. The activities were very basic but they focused on helping Aaliyah become aware of, recognize and comprehend environmental sounds and our voices. One activity included ringing a bell and pointing out the sound to Aaliyah. As we did this we would say and sign the word bell. Another activity involved playing with a ball in which we would focus on saying and signing the word ball. No matter what the activity was, the key was repetition. Along with these activities we were also plugged into a great correspondence course through the John Tracy Clinic. Now you can download these courses by going to www.jtc.org or contact the John Tracy Clinic in Los Angeles, CA at 213-748-5481.

The correspondence course was broken up into the baby course for parents of children less than 18 months and then the Preschool course for parents of children 18 months through five years. The correspondence courses were designed to guide parents in helping their hearing-impaired child develop language and auditory awareness. There were many great activities to work on in the correspondence course. Once the activities were completed, we sent a report to the clinic and they would reply with feedback and suggestions. Here is the first letter dated December 11, 1995 that was sent to me after completing activities from the correspondence course.

Dear Andre and Corinne:

I was very pleased to get your application and checklist, and have now sent you the first lesson. You are now enrolled in our Baby Course. Lesson Two should be arriving within a few weeks. Send in your report on Lesson One about four weeks from the date that you receive our materials. When I receive your report, I'll send you Lesson Three so that you will always have one lesson that you're working on, and the next one ready and waiting.

Aaliyah is very young. Take your time to read and reread the lessons. Then, gradually introduce one game at a time starting perhaps with "Quit Talk." You will find techniques learned in one game will apply to other activities. Most importantly, you will gradually incorporate the techniques you have learned through the games into your daily routine with your child.

What good news it was to learn that Aaliyah has her hearing aids. Since they are the ear-level type, you will want to know that there has been publicity about the danger of children swallowing the button-type batteries in hearing aids, watches and calculators. If your child should swallow a battery, your own medical background will be invaluable, Corinne. However, you might want to post near your phone some emergency numbers in case you are not there. You might list the numbers of your local poison control center, your pediatrician or the National Button Battery Ingestion Hotlines – (202) 625-3333 (voice) or (202) 362-8563 (TTY).

With her hearing aids, Aaliyah will be getting the amplification she needs to learn about the world of sound and speech. It will take time for her to learn that sounds and vibrations have been meaning, especially those of the human voice. This is an important part of her learning. Whenever possible, hold Aaliyah and talk in a moderate voice about four or five inches from the microphone about something of interest. Aaliyah will be able to feel the vibrations of your voice throughout her body. Doing this will help to develop Aaliyah's listening skills. Your goal is for your child to wear amplification all her waking hours.

Thank you for mentioning that Aaliyah had her last hearing evaluation this past September. As ongoing testing occurs and copies of her hearing evaluations become available to you, please share them with me. The information will be helpful as I respond to your reports and letters.

It is fortunate that someone from the Childnet Program comes to your home to work with Aaliyah. This should not only help Aaliyah but greatly benefit you as well. We feel strongly that parents are the most important facilitators of their child's learning, and that supportive information can guide the direction of their efforts. I encourage you to coordinate our ideas and suggestions with those given you by the person with your child. As you learn, Aaliyah will learn.

Remember to use every opportunity to talk, talk, and talk, to Aaliyah. Take time or extra steps if necessary to show her the object or action you're talking about. To understand what words mean, she needs something with which to associate them. Pour in language now and someday the giving back will begin.

Return your report or a letter in four or five weeks. If you would find it more convention to call and report on the lessons, please use our toll-free line, 1-800-522-4582 (V/TTY). Whether you write or call, I'll be looking forward to hearing from you. My very good wishes to you and Aaliyah for a happy and healthy holiday season.

Sincerely,
Director of Correspondence Education

After months of learning sign language, appointments with her doctor and audiologist, and working on developing Aaliyah's listening skills we were ready for a vacation. It can be so draining on a family to focus only on meeting the needs of the child with a hearing-impairment. That's why it's necessary to take frequent vacations to maintain a certain level of wellness and sanity. Families need to just get away and enjoy each other's company without focusing on the disability.

The summer after Aaliyah's first birthday we decided to go the Disney World. This was truly a vacation well deserved and we had so much fun. Since we had some basic sign language skills under our belts, we tested our abilities on rides, at restaurants and around the hotel. The experience of signing out in public was very enjoyable and interesting. All of our encounters were positive and were met by people who were curious. People would ask us questions when they saw us sign. Most of the time they would ask "Is she deaf?" "Was she born deaf?" "Does she talk?" "What are those?" (pointing to Aaliyah's hearing aids). Some comments we heard included: "It must be quiet at your house." "I know some sign language see A B C's" or "She doesn't look deaf." I have yet to figure this one out. I must have missed the class on how to spot a deaf person in a crowd. This vacation was wonderful and I will treasure those memories as long as my mind is able. Aaliyah on the other hand doesn't remember going to Disney World and only knows about the vacation through pictures and our stories. She doesn't even remember being terrified of Mickey Mouse as we tried to get a picture. Parents trust me on this one when I say don't take your child to Disney World unless they are over six years old or you know for a fact that their memory is great. What's the point of going somewhere if you are not going to remember being there?

Chapter 5

Relocating for Services

In the fall of 1996, Aaliyah was over one year old and we continued to receive weekly early intervention services in our home. Our sign language vocabulary was growing and she was wearing her hearing aids more often but not all day. Since she was not wearing her hearing aids all day, I felt like a failure as a parent. I assumed that after 12 months she would be wearing them all day. What was I thinking? I set myself up for failure because I didn't set more realistic goals. Once I realized this I did set more realistic goals by setting aside times of the day that would provide the most environmental stimulation for Aaliyah to wear her hearing aids. We chose mornings and afternoons right after she woke up because it was during these times that she was the most awake and there were plenty of things going on such as meal time and playtime. It can be very frustrating trying to keep hearing aids on young children but again I would really encourage parents to be patient and set realistic goals. The day will come when your child will wear the aids all day. For Aaliyah that day came when she was three and going to preschool. Don't expect your child to wear the hearing aids all day once they get them because it just won't happen. You are setting yourself up to feel like a failure like I did. If your child pulls the hearing aids off, be consistent on how you handle this and soon your child will realize that pulling the hearing aids off is not an option. A technique I used with Aaliyah was distracting her by giving her a toy as I put the aids back on.

As Aaliyah got older and closer to preschool age, I began to worry about her attending school in the area because the educational options were poor for deaf and hard of hearing children, as I had mentioned in an earlier chapter. My worries were somewhat alleviated one day at work when I came across a family who was being "compassionately reassigned." This meant that a soldier was being reassigned to a military base closer to his ill mother so he could care for her. I was very curious to find out which situations qualified for compassionate reassignments and when I had asked Aaliyah's pediatrician he said that our situation definitely qualified. If Aaliyah were to get a cochlear implant than she would need to be near a large Army medical facility that would be able to perform the operation and follow up care including audiological and speech therapy services.

I was truly excited to find out that we were being given an opportunity to move to an area that would provide more services for Aaliyah. As soon as I told my husband of the news, he picked Aaliyah up and gave her a big hug and kiss. I believe his exact words at the time were "Thank you baby, you are my ticket out of here." I think I even saw a tear in his eye because he was so happy (although he will never admit to that). You see he was not very fond of this particular military assignment and I think he felt somewhat short changed since this was his second time being stationed in Louisiana. I liked the area even though you had to drive one hour to the nearest mall and the most exciting thing the area saw was the opening of a 24-hour Super Wal-Mart. We were about one hour from Texas, about four hours from New Orleans, and 8-10 hours from Florida. Ft. Polk was located between two very small cities called Leesville and De Ridder. When asked how I dealt with the heat in Louisiana, I replied that I rarely felt the heat because I was never outside. I went from my air-conditioned house to my air-conditioned car and then to my air-conditioned work.

The day after my husband got the information about the "compassionate reassignment," he worked quickly at getting the paper work together. One part of the process was to fill out a military dream sheet or wish list. The military allowed him to put down three locations where he would like to be stationed so we asked the early intervention specialist to investigate which cities with major military installations provided services for families with deaf children. She contacted Gallaudet University, the world's only Liberal Arts University for Deaf and Hard of Hearing Students located in Washington, D.C. and they recommended Washington State. Along with Gallaudet's recommendations, I researched the reference issue published by the American Annals of the Deaf. This resource definitely came in handy and I would definitely encourage every family moving to a new city to subscribe by calling 1-202-651-5488 (V/TTY).

The annual reference issue provided us with a comprehensive listing, which included contact names, addresses and telephone numbers of schools and programs in the United States and Canada for students who are deaf and hard of hearing. It also listed program information about the schools, services offered within the schools, and mode of communication used by the schools. The three different types of schools that offer programs to deaf and hard of hearing students described in the issue included oral, residential and public schools with a Deaf and Hard of Hearing Program.

Oral schools are private schools, which offer mostly day programs, some residential, and some both. They provide services to children from infancy to high school age and are dedicated to educating deaf and hard-of-hearing children through the auditory-oral approach with emphasis on auditory training, speech production, and speech reading. An informative Web site for oral deaf education is www.oraldeafed.org.

The oral school's philosophy is that regardless of the severity of a child's hearing loss, that child can learn to listen and communicate orally without relying on sign language. The ultimate goals of these programs are designed to prepare students for success in mainstream school placement as early as possible. In general these schools provide the following programs: Early Intervention, Preschool, Mainstream, Speech and Language services, Audiological Services, Cochlear Implant services, Counseling, and Parent Support groups. Most of these schools charge tuition. However, they make every effort to make financial aid available to the parents enrolling their children in one of these programs. Financial aid scholarships are available and amounts vary with the different programs. Fortunately for many parents, through the Individualized Education Program (IEP) process, local school districts accept the financial responsibility for a child with special needs, transferring public funds to the private auditory-oral school program. Many if not all of these programs state that no child has been turned away from these programs because of parents' inability to pay. Two sources for financial assistance for oral deaf education include the Alexander Graham Bell Association for the Deaf and Hard of Hearing, located in Washington D.C. (202-337-5220) and The Geoffrey Foundation located in Kennebunkport, ME (207-967-5798).

Most schools for the deaf in the U.S. are residential schools and therefore the children live on campus. These schools service children anywhere from birth to 22. They have set schedules when the children come home to visit. For example, one school's schedule may have home visits every weekend while another school may have home visits every third weekend. There are a few residential schools in Massachusetts, New York, Pennsylvania, Rhode Island and Wyoming that offer day programs. Most schools for the deaf do not require tuition from families. Lastly, the issue listed public schools that have a Deaf and Hard of Hearing Program, which may be either an oral program or a total communication program.

After we gathered as much information as we could about where to move, we narrowed our choices to three cities: Ft. Lewis, WA, Ft. Leonard Wood, MO and Ft. Sam Houston in San Antonio, TX. All of these cities had a lengthy list of programs for the deaf and I felt that whichever city we moved to would be a definite plus for Aaliyah. Although the military was kind enough to let us put three choices for duty assignments, "the needs of the military came first." I became very familiar with this phrase while I served in the military. This meant that from our three choices, the military would send us to a duty station that needed Andre' the most. My heart was set on Washington based on the recommendation from Gallaudet University so the waiting game was on.

In December of 1996, the day finally arrived when Andre' received orders to report to his new duty assignment at Ft. Lewis, Washington on February 24, 1997. We could not have asked for a better Christmas present. Although I had become very comfortable with our life in Leesville, Louisiana, I was looking forward to moving to a big city. I envisioned many resources for the deaf and a large selection of school programs. Finally, a place where my name was not "Honey" and the police were not named "Bubba."

January 1997 was upon us and it was going to be a great year. The moving company came to our home and packed all of our household goods. The movers were than going to transport our belongings to Washington where they would be placed in military storage until we made arrangements for them to be delivered to our new home. After moving out of our home we stayed at the military guesthouse for a couple of weeks. This time allowed Andre' to finish his paperwork that the military required prior to moving to a new duty assignment and for us to prepare for our long journey. We estimated that the trip would take 2-3 days and our travel route included driving through Texas, New Mexico, Arizona, up the California coast, Oregon, and the southern part of Washington.

Overall, the drive went well and Aaliyah did much better than I had expected. On day two of our trip, the car Andre' drove started to overheat because the radiator needed to be fixed. Eventually, we made it back on the road and finally arrived at Ft. Lewis, Washington on February 6, 1997. We were overcome with feelings of excitement, exhaustion and happiness. Finally we were somewhere that we could call home for awhile.

Chapter 6

Welcome to Washington

Our long journey finally came to an end when we approached the gate to Ft. Lewis. We asked the guards to give us directions to the guesthouse, which would be our temporary home. Our room at the guesthouse consisted of two queen size beds, a couch, a table and a bathroom. There was a little play area outside in the backyard for the children. We didn't have a kitchen area in our room so we had to use the community kitchen where we were able to prepare gourmet meals such as ala lunch bucket and ala hungry man. We also had a community laundry room. Living in one room with a two year old was very challenging and even though we brought a lot of toys, we still went stir crazy. At times the halls and lobby became an extension of our room to the objection of some of the other patrons at the guesthouse. I could almost guarantee that these individuals didn't have children.

Most of the families we met at the guesthouse were very friendly. Many of them were there temporarily while their children had major operations and others were being stationed at Ft. Lewis just like us. Meeting with these families definitely put my feelings about Aaliyah's deafness in perspective. These families had children who were having open-heart surgery or who had cancer and my beautiful daughter was healthy. What did I have to be sad about, nothing, absolutely nothing?

Although we were happy to get settled, a few days after arriving at the base, I found myself buried under feelings of uncertainty. There were so many questions running through my head. Would I be able to find a job that met my family's needs? Would there be enough services available to meet Aaliyah's needs? Overall, would this be the best place for our family to settle in?

After living out of our hotel room for more than one month, we were definitely ready to move into something bigger and permanent. Andre' was just about to start his new job and I needed to find work. I never had to go job hunting before because straight from college, I went into the

Army as a nurse and worked in military hospitals. I didn't think it would be hard finding a job, maybe four or five days tops. What was I thinking? I focused on the hospitals in the area since that's what I had experience in. Every day I drove to at least 2-3 hospitals turning in resume' after resume' only to get the infamous response of "Sorry, we are not hiring at this time but we will keep your application and resume' on file for six months. One week had gone by and I was beside myself. What was I going to do? I could not believe that finding a job was taking so long and I began to feel depressed. I don't think that I was at a point where I would have been clinically diagnosed yet.

In the midst of job hunting, we also started to look for a place to live. During the military's orientation classes for families who were new to the area we were given information on the good and bad areas to live in. We decided to go apartment hunting first, however, soon realized that the amount of money we would be paying in rent was equivalent to a mortgage payment so we switched our focus on purchasing a home.

Our real estate agent was a real go-getter and he was determined to find us a home. After showing us a few homes, we realized that in order for us to afford a home in Washington both of us would need to work. Our three-bedroom two full bath home in Louisiana would have sold for about $74,000, whereas a home the same size here was going for $150,000. We told our agent that we would not be able to purchase a home until I had a job. Well, no sooner than we said that, he pulled out his laptop and began surfing the net for nursing jobs. The day after this meeting, he introduced us to a co-worker whose wife worked in a pediatric clinic and I was given a contact name to call. I was a little hesitant at first because I had never worked in this type of setting before but I was on that phone pronto and I had an interview scheduled the next day with the nurse manager. The day after the interview I was offered a job. I was elated because finally after two weeks of job hunting, I hit the jackpot.

Our lives were falling into place and now we only had two major goals to work on. One goal was to get Aaliyah hooked up with services within the community and the second goal was to find a house to live in. When I accepted the job at the pediatric clinic, I took a decrease in pay but it really didn't matter because it allowed me to have the perfect schedule for Aaliyah. As parents we have to work around our child's schedule and make some sacrifices. It's well worth it in the end when we see how successful our children have become.

The military was very quick to assign Aaliyah to the Developmental Pediatric Clinic at Madigen Army Medical Center (MAMC). All children who had developmental needs were assigned to this clinic, while children without development needs were assigned to a regular pediatric clinic.

During Aaliyah's first appointment at MAMC we were once again told to consider a cochlear implant and were referred to an ENT doctor and a Speech Pathologist. We saw the ENT specialist that same day and he recommended that we get a Bone CT scan done and a sedated ABR in preparation for a cochlear implant. Just like the unwritten motto of the military to "Hurry up and wait" I guess the ENT specialist thought he would rush to get all these tests done and wait for our decision regarding the implant. However, it was a topic that we'd thrown around so I was glad that we were getting this done. If anything came back abnormal that would have been the deciding factor against pursuing the implant.

Once the medical appointments for Aaliyah were initiated, it was only a matter of a couple of weeks before we were connected with the local school district's Parent Infant Program for the Deaf/Hard of Hearing or PIP as it was called. The program had a parent Infant Specialist, who worked in a similar capacity as the Early Intervention Specialist in Louisiana. The PIP program involved weekly home visits by the Parent Infant Specialist and attending the PIP class at Birney Elementary School once a week.

Our initial meeting with the Parent Infant Specialist was in our room at the guesthouse but shortly thereafter we found a house that we wanted to purchase. It was located close to the military base and my new job. It was situated in a Cul-de-sac with a huge back yard that was fenced in. This house and neighborhood was perfect for us because Aaliyah would be able to play outside in the backyard without us worrying about her wondering off.

The neighborhood was quiet and there was hardly any traffic but some of our neighbors told us that sometimes drivers drove fast into the Cul-de-sac as they turned around. As a result about one month after moving into our house we looked into placing a street sign as you entered the Cul-de-sac. This would inform drivers to drive slowly because there is a deaf child at play. I contacted the county's Public Works and Utilities and was told to go to a sign place to have the sign made based on specifications given to us by the county. Some counties and cities will pay for the sign but the county we lived in didn't so we were responsible for paying for it. Also, we were told to go around to our neighbors and as a courtesy let them know that we would be placing a sign in the area which may or may not be in front of their property. One house that was situated as you entered the street that led into our Cul-de-sac informed us that they did not want the sign, which would have been on the side of their property and not in front. We told them that we were not asking for permission and according to the county could place the sign where we wanted (although a county official would need to make the final decision). The woman that lived in the house told me "if you keep your deaf child in the house than you don't have to worry about the sign. She shouldn't be playing outside anyway since she can't hear the cars." I angrily told the woman that she was insensitive and stupid to make such a suggestion and that we would put the sign in the best place and if that meant on the side of their property (which was actually county property) than so be it. None of the other homes in the neighborhood had a problem with the sign and eventually we put it up a few feet before you actually turned into the Cul-de-sac, which didn't end up being near the home of the "idiot." We never did talk to those people the whole time we lived in that house.

Hanging out, Aaliyah and Dad, Summer 1997

First summer in Washington, Aaliyah and Mom, 1997

Wow, we found a house to live in, Aaliyah got connected to services within the community, and I found a job for myself all within two months of moving to Washington. My work hours were Monday through Friday in the evenings and one or two Saturdays a month while André would be working Monday through Friday from 9-6. Although my work schedule allowed me to take Aaliyah to any appointment or preschool class she might have had during the day, there was about two hours every day that overlapped between the time I left for work and the time André came home from work. We needed to find childcare and so our search began.

We contacted the Child Care Referral Line, which provided information on daycare providers in the area. We were given four names of day care providers who claimed to have experience with special needs children and knew sign language. After interviewing the providers in their homes, we eventually decided to go with a woman whose in-home daycare was close to the military base. She claimed that she and her daughter knew sign language and I took them for their word. One evening after I brought Aaliyah to her, she asked me how to sign some very basic words like eat and drink. Well, it was at this point that I figured out that she didn't know sign language and her skills were limited to the ABC's. She did have one book with basic signs for childcare providers. Her definition of "knowing sign language" and my definition were totally different. A childcare provider would not talk with a hearing baby using only ABC's so why would they think that ABC's for a deaf baby is sufficient language. One word explains this, IGNORANCE!

Although the childcare providers sign skills were poor, she didn't have a lot of children in her daycare was able to give Aaliyah more one on one attention. She was willing to take the time to find out what Aaliyah wanted and learn some basic signs. She did activities with the children and she was a great cook. She was an older woman who worked well with the children and had a lot of patience. She seemed like the perfect surrogate grandparent.

Once again I can't stress enough the importance to really interview the childcare provider thoroughly to include their sign language ability. While interviewing, sign with the provider to see exactly what she knows and understands. However, ultimately you want someone who will take great care of your child and one whom your child likes. Even though a childcare provider may know sign language fluently, doesn't mean that the person will work out any better. I learned this from an experience we had with a deaf childcare provider.

I thought I had found the ultimate childcare provider because she would understand how to communicate with Aaliyah at a level that a hearing person could not. I thought I had hit pay dirt. Actually, I think the provider hit pay dirt. She was the only deaf childcare provider in the area and I think if a parent really had their mind set on hiring her they would be willing to pay any price. I felt that she used the situation to her advantage and therefore her prices were a little bit more than the other daycares. She kept a clean home, had rules, and was very into arts and crafts.

Overall, she seemed caring yet stern and initially, Aaliyah didn't mind going to her. It was only on Fridays after school, school breaks and a few days during the week in the summer. However, once summer finished and Aaliyah went back to her on Fridays, she would cry every now and then all the way there. As a result there were a few times I brought Aaliyah to my job until her dad could get her because I didn't have the heart to drop her off at the providers house. I asked Aaliyah if the provider was mean to her and she said no. When I asked her why she didn't want to go to the provider's house she told me "I want to be with you." I also found out from Aaliyah, that the provider would run a lot of errands while watching Aaliyah which I couldn't understand since Aaliyah was the only child in her day care at the time. This meant that Friday for a few hours was the only day she had a child in her day care and for some strange reason she had to schedule all her errands at that time. Well, I quickly put a stop to that. She had tried numerous times to convince me to bring Aaliyah to her more than once a week because she said that Aaliyah was having a hard time adjusting to her. I told the provider that my goal was not to have Aaliyah in childcare at all and if she only had to be in childcare 2-3 hours a week I felt that I was being somewhat successful in meeting my goal.

After a while, she began bothering us about payments-which were never late. She would call me at work and tell me we were short a couple of bucks or request that we pay her two months in advance since that is what most day cares do. I always made sure that I double-checked what she was due and paid her accordingly. I also called the licensing agency and was told that this was not a set policy by all childcare providers to request payment two months in advance. One time she told André "Even though you bring Aaliyah to me from 3:30 to 6:30 I will have to charge you from the top of the hour since that is what most day cares do." When I asked her for clarification, she said "Andre' misunderstood me, that is not what I said." Another time she corrected me rather rudely about calling her a baby-sitter. We were discussing something when I had called her a baby-sitter. She angrily said, "I am not a baby-sitter. You are a baby-sitter, and I am a childcare provider." I explained to her that I did not know the sign for a childcare provider and that's why I called her a baby-sitter.

Well, I abruptly ended our conversation and took Aaliyah home because that was the last straw. She made me so angry that I quickly found a replacement for her. André and I felt like she was more interested in getting our money instead of taking care of our daughter. Shortly after our childcare issue was resolved, André started his job. We finally moved into our home and were becoming more involved with the early intervention programs.

The Parent Infant Specialist, who came to our home once a week, was a wonderful sounding board and a great resource. One concern I shared with her was Aaliyah's hearing aid usage. She assured me that there were other parents out there who had the same problem and that I was doing a great job. It was an awesome feeling to have someone tell me this. I am not the kind of person that needs to be showered with accolades but every now and then I savor them when it happens. The days that she came to our home we worked on building my communication skills and Aaliyah's listening skills. One activity involved playing with a drum. We sat on the floor and positioned Aaliyah's back toward the drum. As the Parent Infant Specialist banged the drum, I would turn Aaliyah to face her. In essence we were training Aaliyah to respond to sounds. As hearing individuals we automatically turn our head when we hear sounds or our name being called. Children with hearing impairments need to be trained to do the same because it is not automatic for them. These visits and activities were a nice continuation of the services we got in Louisiana.

Attending the parent infant program at the school was my chance to talk with other parents who were dealing with similar issues as myself. The class allowed me to see how other deaf children interact with each other as well as their parents. This was a great experience and all of the parents were very enthusiastic to be there for the children. The class agenda included playtime, circle time, snack time, and playtime again while the parents met for a group discussion. At these discussions we would learn about the different sign language classes being offered, what types of services other parents came across, places to get sign language material, and when and where there may be activities that families with deaf and hard of hearing children could attend.

Interacting with the other parents really helped me feel that I was not alone in my worries about how to take care of a child and that I was doing a great job. We were a great resource for each other except for one parent, who had a way of making me feel that I was not doing enough. She would spew information constantly whether I wanted to know about it or not. She would make me feel like I should have been doing more for Aaliyah, perhaps crusading down the streets of the capital. She would often start conversations with "Did you know about this or that." or "I really fought for this or that." She would never wait to be asked questions. She would never start a conversation "How are Aaliyah and you doing?" She tried to dominate a lot of the group discussions, which made me feel inadequate. We all try to do what is best for our children so it really nauseates me to have to deal with parents who try to make me feel less of a parent because I may not have known something that they knew or perhaps they do not agree with my philosophy in raising my daughter. It was for that reason that I pretty much avoided this mom, although the other moms seemed drawn to her or perhaps she forced her presence onto them.

I found it interesting that this mother spent a lot of her energy becoming immersed in the Deaf culture. That's great but her child was a toddler and really not old enough to become an active participant in the Deaf culture. She also began to learn American Sign Language and made it a point to let the other parents know that this was the language of the Deaf and was in essence better to know than Signing Exact English, which is what I was learning. I strongly believed that my most important job at the time was to help Aaliyah learn language through communication while becoming immersed in the Deaf culture would be focused on later. Our children can't be successful members of any culture if they can't communicate. By the way, years later I met up with this mom at the gymnastic center Aaliyah attended. She was actually really nice to talk with this time because she asked how we were doing, didn't make it a point to talk about her battles and even commented on how obsessed she had been in the past about ASL but now was looking into Signing Exact English.

Communication is the exchange of information, ideas and feelings between people. People exchange information through facial expression, body language, gestures, speech, sign language, reading and writing. Communicating involves two processes: sending information and receiving information. The person sending information expresses ideas or information or feelings. The person receiving the message understands the ideas or information or feelings that have been expressed. In order to communicate, people need to learn to use language. Also, the sender and the receiver must understand each other.

Language is the use of particular words in a particular order to convey meaning. In order to teach Aaliyah language, we needed to help her learn the signs for particular words and meanings which was accomplished by signing and saying the words or ideas many, many times. Repetition was the key to Aaliyah's language development. A hearing child may only need to hear a word a few hundred times before they begin to understand the word while a deaf child needs to have the word repeated at least 1000 times before they understand the word. I began to keep a list of words that I knew Aaliyah understood because she would sign them without my help or prompting. It was exciting to see this list grow.

Along with developing Aaliyah's language, it was also important for us to focus on developing her listening skills. I had hoped that since she wore her hearing aids more often she was on the road to hearing some sounds. Hearing-impaired children develop their listening skills the same way that hearing children do. They go through three major stages: awareness, recognition, and comprehension.

Ideally, Aaliyah would need to learn to understand certain things about sound before she could move onto the next developmental level. First in order to know that she was aware of sounds we observed her for responses such as blinking, stopping movement for an instant, or trying to see what made the sound. Once she was aware of sounds then she could begin to pay more attention to the same sounds that she heard again and again. Eventually, she would begin to notice that every sound is different which meant that she began to recognize sounds. One of the first sounds a baby recognizes is his mother's voice.

Finally, once Aaliyah realized that some sounds meant something in particular then she was one step toward comprehending sound. One of the most complex sounds a baby learns to comprehend is the series of sounds we call speech. When a baby comprehends speech sounds then he has developed receptive language. Memory is involved in the recognition and comprehension of speech. If a baby can't remember having heard a sound before, he cannot learn to recognize or comprehend it unless it is repeated. It took so long to see results that I had to frequently tell myself "Be patient Corinne, Aaliyah has to learn to use what little hearing she has and this could take awhile."

Along with the Parent and Infant Program, I also found other valuable community resources. I connected with Washington PAVE, a non-profit organization whose staff was primarily made up of parents who had children with special needs. They were wonderful in providing information on how to understand the educational system particularly with IFSP's and IEP's. My resources did not stop here.

I had been given a list of community resources that listed four other early intervention programs. The contact person listed for these programs was called a Family Resource Coordinator (FRC), who is responsible for accessing and coordinating early intervention services including screenings, developmental preschools, SSI, and health services for families with children with developmental concerns birth to three. Basically, the FRC's job is to ensure that families understand the services available within the community. Our FRC was wonderful. She told us about assistive devices for the Deaf that we could get for free through the early intervention program. The devices she helped us get included a signal light for the doorbell and telephone, and a vibrating alarm clock. I felt that adapting our home environment was the next logical step in helping Aaliyah become more independent and feel that everyone in the family was equally important. I wanted our home to help facilitate Aaliyah's communication as well as help her become aware of her surroundings.

Not only were these assistive devices great for Aaliyah but for us as well. When we were outside or vacuuming in the house and the telephone or doorbell rang, we could see the flashing lights, which were especially noticeable when all the lights were off. Although Aaliyah was too young to really use the vibrating clock, I was going to get all the assistive devices I could before the services provided through the early intervention program stopped when she turned three. These devices were and are not cheap. In order to get this equipment free, we had to get at least three letters from Aaliyah's health care team and then give them to our FRC. We received one letter from the Audiologist, one from the Speech Therapist, and one from the Ear, Nose, and Throat Specialist.

Along with paying for these devices the Early Intervention Program paid for a Signing Exact English conference that was one week long. This was a great conference put on by the SEE Center and childcare was provided so our whole family was able to attend. The first day of the conference focused primarily on finding out what level each person was at and once this was established, the rest of the conference centered on building vocabulary. Each class had to learn the signs to a song and put on a little skit at the end of the conference. André and I were in the same class and our song was "Down by the Bay." André wore dread locks and represented a Jamaican man while the rest of the class wore watermelon hats. The skit involved all of us sitting in front of the stage singing, signing, and swaying while André danced around behind us. It was quite funny and needless to say André was the hit of the skit as well as the class. The children in the daycare with Aaliyah also worked on a song. It was adorable to see all the children try to sign and sing in unison.

There was one day during the conference that we were not allowed to talk. On this day, André, Aaliyah, and I went to Mc Donald's for lunch and before we went inside, André wrote on a piece of paper "I would like a number 4". Somehow, I don't think this is what the instructors had in mind. This conference was so much fun that I would strongly recommend any family with a Deaf or Hard of Hearing child to attend. Being immersed in sign language for a full week gives you just a taste of what your deaf child goes through on a daily basis. It was very educational, interesting, hard, fun, and inspiring.

Lastly, our FRC coordinated with our school district to pay for an interpreter for Aaliyah while attending a preschool class with hearing children and to come to our home and teach us sign language once every other week. If you have a hearing-impaired child from birth to three and you don't have a Family Resource Coordinator, find one. This person will be a wonderful resource for your family. As I surfed the web on the topic of FRC's, I found that many states use the same term. To find an FRC in the state of Washington contact WithinReach (formerly Healthy Mothers, Healthy Babies), at 1-800-322-2588 /TTY relay: 711. This statewide number provides information and referral to resources within the state. It also connects families to local Family Resource Coordinators. If a family does not live in the state of Washington and would like to find an FRC, I would recommend that parents contact their state's Early Intervention Program, the school district in which they reside, the child's doctor office, or the Department of Health.

After I had contacted two of the other early intervention programs on the community resource list, I toured their facilities. I spoke with the teachers who were in charge of the preschool classes, and the FRCs involved with both programs. I thought it would be a great balance to have Aaliyah be a part of a preschool class with Deaf children and one with hearing children. One of the programs I examined had a great schedule with playtime, circle time, and parent group discussion. There was also an Occupational and Speech Therapist on site that would work with the children that needed this service. However, the facility where this program took place was cramped and there was not a lot of room for the children to strengthen their gross motor skills.

The other program took place in a larger facility. There was a big back yard and a gym for the children to play in. Their schedule consisted of playtime, story time, snack time and no parent discussion group. After investigating these two programs I eventually decided to go with the program that had the bigger facility. We attended this preschool program once a week and Aaliyah was the only deaf child in the group while some of the other children had language delays. It was wonderful to see that she got along with all the hearing children. She never sat in the corner and watched the other children play. She was right there where the action was. Her sense of sight has always been very sharp because she has been very alert at what is happening around her. My husband attributes this to being female and insists that it is the female nature to be "Nosey." However, if there is anything going on in the neighborhood he seems to be the first one at the window to check things out.

After a few weeks of attending this group, I was beginning to feel that Aaliyah was not getting a lot out of the story time sessions because the teacher didn't know sign language. How could she know what was being said without sign language. What was I thinking? As strange as it may sound, it was very easy to forget that Aaliyah was deaf by the way she interacted with the other children. The children talked with her as if she was just one of the children talking in their own language-Kidgiberish. They had no idea that she could not hear. I guess I got caught up with enjoying my little girl interacting with others and did not really pay attention to what she could be missing in the classroom.

I informed our FRC about my concerns related to what Aaliyah was missing in the classroom. She informed me that it was our school district's responsibility to provide a sign language interpreter for this preschool class. The FRC stated that at the time she didn't know of anyone available but would look into the interpreter registry and find someone. She asked if I had anyone in mind but since I was fairly new to the area, I didn't. As luck would have it one week after this discussion, I met a mother who had brought her sick children to the pediatric office I worked at. You may ask what does this have to do with interpreters. Well, she turned out to be a certified interpreter.

"Ann" had just moved to the area and was looking for a job. After talking with her, I felt that Aaliyah would love her as an interpreter. She was from the south and had a very sweet and polite disposition. I gave her the name of our FRC and asked if she would call her to talk about interpreting for Aaliyah at her preschool class with the hearing children. She was definitely over qualified for a preschool class but she was willing to start there and I am happy she did. It was only about one or two days later that I received a call from our FRC to let us know that she had hired "Ann" and that she would be there for Aaliyah's next class.

The first day at preschool having an interpreter was amazing and quite enlightening for the teacher. While she was singing Twinkle, Twinkle, Little Star to the children she was making hand movements that she herself was probably taught as a child. Well, "Ann" nearly fell over in shock as she watched and interpreted the song because after the song was over she had to quietly correct the teacher on her hand movements. You see the teacher was making a hand movement for star that was actually the sign for vagina. The teacher had to make some adjustments in her teaching style especially when it came time to singing songs. She also had to be more aware of where Aaliyah was sitting because she needed to sit up front so that she could see the interpreter as well as the teacher. However, at this age Aaliyah focused on the interpreter and rarely looked at the teacher. Matter of fact, all of the children focused on the interpreter's hand movements.

The interpreter worked well with this age group and spent most of the class time on the floor at eye level with the children. All the children were drawn to her and no matter where Aaliyah was, "Ann" was right there interpreting what was going on. She would interpret everything that was being said in class, which made me feel that we were making the most of this experience. A few months later the school district paid for "Ann" to come to our home once every other week to teach André and I sign language. We were very lucky to have her teach us sign language and to be Aaliyah's interpreter. Soon she was in such demand that her schedule was full and eventually she had to cut back on interpreting and since has moved to another state.

Aaliyah continued to have a full schedule in the early intervention programs. She attended preschool classes twice a week and the Parent Infant Specialist came to our home once a week. I was very happy we moved to Washington and pleased with the services we were receiving.

Aaliyah playing dress up

Aaliyah the "Good Witch" for
Halloween 1999

Chapter 7

Speech Therapy for Aaliyah

Starting speech therapy for Aaliyah was an area I didn't know much about. When would she be ready? The early intervention specialist in Louisiana said that Aaliyah could start speech therapy once her babbling began to have a pattern and a rhythm to it. As much as I would like to say I was in tune with Aaliyah, her babbling sounded the same to me at any stage. Would she benefit from speech therapy at this point if we didn't know how much benefit she was getting from her hearing aids? On the other hand, I didn't want to wait too long, passing crucial developmental stages. Answering the above questions is not easy but one thing is for certain the earlier a child receives early intervention services including speech therapy, the stronger the child's language and communication skills will be. A few months before Aaliyah turned two, her new pediatrician referred her to a speech pathologist.

A Speech-Language Pathologists (SLP) is educated in human communication, including its development and disorders. They are trained to help children and adults who have problems with speech and language develop effective communication skills. When searching for the appropriate SLP for your child it is important to consider their level of education. An SLP working in private practice should have a master's degree in speech-language pathology. The letters M.S., M.A. or M. Ed. after their name signify the SLP holds a master's degree. A master's degree requires two years of intensive training and supervised clinical practice in the field following obtaining a bachelor's degree. Some public school systems allow an SLP to practice with a bachelor's degree (B.S. or B.A.). While a clinician at the bachelor's degree level possesses general, introductory knowledge of speech-language pathology, the additional experience obtained at the master's level is necessary to be considered a certified SLP by the American Speech-Language-Hearing Association (ASHA). This Certificate of Clinical Competence is indicated by a CCC-S next to the degree level. For example, you may see something like Jane Doe, MS CCC-S or Jane Doe, MA CCC-S.L. Along with the educational level of the SLP take into account the experience of that person with hearing-impaired children. If a child has never heard before then the approach to the therapy will be different than a child who can hear but is not speaking correctly. A child's speech is impacted by the degree of hearing loss. For example, the child who lost hearing after birth has heard for some time and will speak better than the child who was born deaf. The child born deaf has never heard speech before and therefore does not have a memory of how speech sounds. Also, make sure that the therapist's communication philosophy meshes with your family's mode of communication. In other words, if your family uses the oral method of communication then obviously you wouldn't want a therapist that signs. The reverse is also true so if your family uses sign language than you would want a therapist that signs.

Prior to Aaliyah's evaluation by an SLP, she had an audiogram done in March of 1997. I was shocked by the audiologist's impression of the results because she felt that Aaliyah was getting little if any benefit from the current hearing aids. A part of me felt that we were wasting our time with the hearing aids but then another part of me said that Aaliyah was just beginning to wear them more often.

After the audiogram, Aaliyah was evaluated by a speech pathologist and her assessment was a no brainer. She stated that when compared with hearing children of the same age, Aaliyah's speech and language development were delayed. Really, what a surprise! According to the therapist's notes she wrote "Aaliyah vocalized to herself several times (“uh”) otherwise, she would not make eye contact with me as I signed to her, nor followed my signed directions as I signed in front of her. Aaliyah recognizes approximately 10 – 15 signs. She follows signed single directions such as "Come," "Sit," and "Give". Her expressive vocabulary includes at least eight signs. She will imitate a few signs, such as "Please." After this evaluation, we were referred to another speech and language pathologist in Tacoma who specialized in speech therapy for individuals with significant hearing impairments and used sign language in her sessions.

On May 29, 1997, Aaliyah had just turned two and began speech therapy three times a week with each session being one hour. The treatment plan for the speech therapy sessions involved the total communication approach, with emphasis on her auditory, articulation, and language skills. The speech therapist was going to work on a number of things. First she wanted to maximize Aaliyah's residual hearing by helping her become aware of sound sources. Second, she wanted to work on Aaliyah's articulation by pairing all signs with verbalization and establishing oral/sign vocabulary. Third, she wanted to encourage Aaliyah to imitate non-speech and speech sounds while tone patterns were established. Lastly, she wanted to work on building Aaliyah's language.

Aaliyah was expected to pair responses and requests with sign and vocalization. She was to increase her vocabulary in categories such as animals, foods, toys, body parts, household items, family members, clothing, and actions. She was to increase her spontaneous use of language, which meant that she was to initiate communication whether it by vocalization or signing to get her wants and needs met. We were told not to let Aaliyah point to what she wanted; instead she was expected to give us a sign and vocalization. I was told that if I did let Aaliyah point to all the things she wanted this would stunt her language development as well as produce frustration when her more complicated needs were not met. I didn't want to have a pointing machine on my hand but most importantly, I didn't want Aaliyah to be frustrated so we really worked hard on her signing and vocalizing. I wouldn't say that we never allowed her to point because she did her fair share of pointing in order to get her needs met. Sometimes it was easier to give her what she wanted when she pointed to the object instead of waiting for her to vocalize.

Aaliyah's language was slowly growing and we had been working on developing her listening skills so now we could begin to concentrate on her speech. I was told that it would be many years before Aaliyah would speak with words that could be understood. At seven, she could say, "Stop it", "I Love You", mom, dad, boat, blue, yellow, green, purple and off. She could say the following sounds "sh", "s", "mm", "oo", "ee" and the following letters K, T, P, M, F and N. I waited 10 years to hear "What is your favorite color or animal?" "Thank you" "Your are beautiful" and "Whatever." I am excited to see her progress in another five years although I may choose not to understand such phrases as "Can I drive the car?" "Mom I have a boyfriend." or "Mom can I get my nose pierced?" - Aaliyah I am telling you now that you can't get any body part pierced except for your ears and no more than 2 holes in each ear. Now that should cover all aspects of piercing.

Speech therapy is not really understood by people who are not involved with it. Most people assume that speech therapy is like a pill that will make people talk. Many people would ask me "Can Aaliyah talk now?" and I would constantly reply, "Aaliyah has always talked but it will be years before we can understand much of her speech without sign language." One important thing I learned from sitting in on Aaliyah's speech therapy sessions in the past and present is that there is more involved than just learning to speak. The main focus of the sessions was to concentrate on building language and maximizing Aaliyah's residual hearing that in turn would help fine tune her lip reading skills. At each session the therapist focused on a group of words and sounds for months. Repeating the words hundreds of times was so important in helping Aaliyah say some of the words that we now understand without her signing.

Although speech for Aaliyah may be harder to master since she was born deaf, I refuse to put limits on what she can or can't do. You will never hear me say, " Aaliyah can't talk because she is deaf" or "Aaliyah can't dance because she is deaf." My mother placed limitations on me when I was younger and it really did affect how successful I thought I could be. An example was when I wanted to be a veterinarian, a dream most kids I think have at one point if they love animals. We always had pets either cats or dogs and even though I was allergic to cats I never remembered having any allergy related problems. However, my mother would always say "How can you be a veterinarian if you are allergic to animals?" She would say this every time I mentioned being a veterinarian and after hearing this so many times I began agreeing with her. Eventually, I convinced myself that I could never become a vet and decided on another career path.

Limitations placed on children can have a negative impact on their self-esteem. If you constantly bombard the child with "you can't do this or that", then they will begin to believe it. I am not about to put such limitations on Aaliyah especially when it comes to speech. If Aaliyah does not speak well after years of speech therapy that will be fine because at least we can say she worked hard and tried her best. A person shouldn't feel like a failure if they have tried their best. Failure is not trying at all. I want to make sure that we nourish and strengthen Aaliyah's self-esteem so that she will look at limitations as goals to achieve. I know that Aaliyah's speech may not be 100% understandable but I hope that with her continued hard work at speech and auditory training that in time most of her speech will be understandable. Her strength and perseverance can only lead to improvement.

Aaliyah's speech therapy was covered until June 1999 by the military and we were only paying $25.00/month based on my husband's rank. After June, Aaliyah was covered under my health insurance plan at work, which was Regence Blue Shield. Boy were we in for a financial shock because my health insurance plan had a $1,000 per year cap on speech therapy coverage and at $66 per hour that only covered 15 sessions per year. The following year the speech therapy cap went to $1,500 per year and the therapy sessions went from $66.00 to $72.00 per hour. I was frustrated that we could not afford the private speech therapist twice a week so I contacted the insurance company. I was told to fill out the appeal procedure form to request a raise in the speech therapy cap from $1,500 to $7,500. This amount would allow Aaliyah to continue her private speech therapy sessions twice a week. Along with the appeal form I obtained a letter from Aaliyah's speech therapist as well as her pediatrician stressing the importance of Aaliyah continuing a minimum of two hours of speech therapy a week. I faxed all this information to the appeals committee and received the following response: "Your request for the increase of speech therapy benefits has been reviewed. Unfortunately, we are unable to increase the level of speech therapy benefits from $1,500 per year to $7,500 per year. Your employer determines your benefits. They choose this particular health plan with these specific limits. We cannot make any changes to the level of benefits". So let me get this straight, the insurance company seems to think it is reasonable to place a limit on the amount of speech therapy covered for a deaf child who did not choose to be deaf. Yet, is very generous in the amount of coverage for an alcoholic or drug addict (who chose to get this way) to get clean. That really makes sense. Let's reward the alcoholics and drug addicts and penalize the individuals who were born with a disability. The cap on speech therapy eventually went up to $2,500 per year and we were responsible for the first $200.00 for the year, which was our deductible. At least these expenses were tax deductible under medical expenses.

I contacted the Department of Health and Social Services and the Social Security Office to see if we could get full or partial medical coverage and Social Security benefits for Aaliyah. However, since my husband and I are productive members of society making a decent income we didn't qualify. Periodically, I check with the system to see if we qualify for services and up to this point we continue to not meet the criteria.

There have been many times I thought about quitting my job so that Aaliyah could get the services she needs. I know that my role as a mother is more important than any career I went to college for. Why don't I quit? I can't give you a good answer. Perhaps societal pressures, for moms to do it all, work and take care of family. It may just boil down to what I was taught while growing up. My mother came from Germany. She grew up on a farm and since she was the oldest daughter, it was her responsibility to help take care of her six other siblings. At times this meant that she had to work for other people outside the farm doing different jobs to make money. She eventually became a seamstress and met my dad. They both came to the United States with little money and her first job was in a clothing factory. She knew no English and struggled to learn the language as well as make it in this country. When I was born she was working as a seamstress in a men's clothing store at the local mall. I remember her always working but being there for us. Her and my dad at times worked opposite shifts or she would take my brother and me to work with her. Occasionally, the neighbors across the street would baby-sit. She seemed to do it all and that is what I learned. You can be a great mom and work as long as you prioritize your children first the rest of "doing it all" falls into place.

Working in a pediatric office, I come across families who really do need assistance from the state to make sure that their children are healthy and get the services they need. However, I have seen my share of "system abuse". Families getting assistance come into the clinic with clothes on that even I could not afford or cell phones of the highest quality. These are the same families that will turn around and call the clinic to request a prescription for over the counter medication such as Tylenol or diapers so that the state pays for it. Frequently, they have a sense of entitlement about them and feel that they must be catered to. It is truly amazing to see these same families unable to take time out of their busy non-working day to follow-up on tests that the doctor felt was necessary for their children even though these test are being paid for by the state. These are the same families who are well enough to get free transportation to and from the appointment but are too ill to ride the bus.

Okay, let me get off of my soapbox. Once I had learned that I could not get any assistance for Aaliyah through the state I was on a mission. I am not sure why I thought this would work but I thought it couldn't hurt to try. Every night for one week, I glued myself to the computer as I searched the Internet for the addresses, phone numbers (most of which I am sure were not accurate) and emails of celebrities. Even though most of the addresses were probably not accurate, I thought I had a small chance of actually having some correct addresses. The individuals I wrote to were actors, actresses (some who were deaf or hard of hearing), singers, talk show hosts (who appeared to be very giving), and even CEO's of some major corporations. In my letter I wrote about my plight regarding lack of funds for Aaliyah's speech therapy and the cap that the insurance company was placing on this service. I thought that some of these individuals would be sympathetic to my plight and offer some financial assistance. Crazy, right but when it comes to my daughter I am not ashamed to ask for help and I had at least 10 pages of names. I only received two replies and these were from the individuals' agents stating that they only gave money to organizations and not to individuals. It was at this time that I vowed I would never give to an organization backed by a celebrity. How hypocritical of them! They will not give to individuals; however, they expect money supporting their cause to come from individuals. Also, they seem to be generous only when the camera is on. I would not give up that easily and had one more idea. I had looked into getting grants for medical expenses. I wrote to at least 10 organizations to inquire about the grants that they had to offer. To my disappointment, I either got responses stating that I lived in the wrong state to qualify for the grant or they did not offer grants for what I was requesting.

Well, the third time was the charm. I knew I was defeated and accepted the fact that there was a cap on these services. The only thing I could do now was to make the most out of our health coverage and work even harder at home with Aaliyah. She continued to receive three hours of speech therapy a week. One session was with her private therapist, another session was with the therapist at Children's hospital and the last session was with her speech therapist in school. In order to avoid going over the speech therapy cap for the year, Aaliyah didn't go to her private speech therapist for the months of July and August but we continued to go to Children's Hospital.

We went to Children's Hospital for speech therapy until Aaliyah was 9 years old and then therapist informed us that she would be moving out of the state. She gave us a couple of options which included continuing to come to Children's Hospital or see another therapist in private practice who also knew sign language. I liked the later option because this therapist had flexible hours which meant that we could go on weekends and Aaliyah wouldn't miss any school.

Chapter 8

Aaliyah's School

After turning three, Aaliyah no longer qualified for services under the Early Intervention Program, now all services would be through the school district. The time for preschool had arrived and I couldn't believe it because she just completed the Parent Infant Program. In any case it was time to move on.

Aaliyah was definitely ready for preschool according to the Parent Infant Specialist who made the following observations of Aaliyah's development up to this point. She was learning how to use her residual hearing through play audiometry and was responding consistently and appropriately to sounds like the large snare drum and tambourine at close range. She was very visually aware of what was happening around her in her environment. Her eye contact skills and ability to look up for information were well. Aaliyah was able to match similar objects, objects by colors and objects to pictures. She used common objects appropriately and understood many descriptive words such as dirty, hot, cold, sleepy, prepositions such as in, out, on, off and action words such as play, eat and drink. She knew some colors when they were named such as red, blue and yellow. Lastly, she knew the names of familiar places such as school and speech. Aaliyah primarily used signs and gestures to communicate her wants and she used her voice with prompting, appropriately and with meaning. Aaliyah used two word sentences spontaneously such as "daddy work." "dog eat." and she imitated three to four word sentences with prompting. She was beginning to answer "what?" and "where?" questions as well as use noun-verb combinations. She imitated finger plays, she commanded others, she was able to take turns and she could name objects in pictures and in the environment.

Based on these observations, the Parent Infant Specialist recommended enrolling Aaliyah in a daily, Total Communication, self-contained preschool for children who are deaf and/or hard-of-hearing. She gave me information and contact names for two preschool programs. The Parent Infant Specialist stressed to us that Aaliyah needed a environment full of language to increase her communication skills with a teacher who had knowledge of working with deaf/hard-of-hearing children and interaction with other deaf and/or hard-of-hearing children.

I really appreciated the information that the Parent Infant Specialist gave me and began to investigate the programs. Preschool A was located in the same school as the PIP program, which was in the Tacoma School District. This was the third largest school district in Washington and contained 53 schools, three of which had a Deaf and Hard of Hearing Program. I was told that this school district had the oldest and one of the best Deaf and Hard of Hearing Programs and other school districts would send deaf and hard of hearing students there. It wasn't until five years prior to moving to Washington, that some of the other school districts developed their own programs, believing that they could meet the needs of the children within their own districts and save money in the process. Preschool B was located in the district we lived in, the Bethel School District.

Although I was already familiar with the building layout and preschool teacher of Preschool A, I was willing to examine the program that Preschool B had to offer. However, I have to admit that I already had my mind set on sending Aaliyah to Preschool A. Ultimately, the following factors helped me decide which program to pick: full day or half day program, class size, the teacher, program philosophy regarding Total Communication and mainstreaming, speech therapy services, audiological services and building layout.

Schools may not want to be classified as childcare but that is exactly what they are. They are responsible for caring for the children in their classroom in the absence of parents. If you were to ask any working parent with school age children what is the hardest part of the school year, I am sure they would say finding childcare for holiday breaks or summer vacation. Since parents with deaf children already have a limited choice of childcare options, it was wonderful to have an all day program as one of our choices in Preschool A. The program was from 8:40 to 2:40, Monday through Friday. The children had a full day but there was also naptime in the afternoon. This program was well established and had been running for many years long before Preschool B started their program.

Preschool B's program was only a few hours long Monday through Thursday because the school district's budget only allowed for a ½ day program. Apparently, many parents preferred this. Some parents felt that an all day program for a preschooler was too long and it was emphasized that what the program lacked in hours made up for in the way the time was spent. For example, I was told that a lot of learning took place during lunchtime where social skills and building vocabulary were stressed. Ideally, that was a nice premise but I wanted a program that had more substance to it.

The second important factor was class size. I felt that a class size of 12 or less would be more conducive to learning and the teacher would be able to pay more attention to all the students. Both schools had about 10 students in their preschool class and I thought this was great. The third factor that had an impact on my decision was the teacher's experience. School A's preschool teacher was deaf. She was born hard of hearing and one day woke up with no hearing so her speech was very good and she was very easy to understand. She had taught at the school for 15 years and I knew she would be a great role model for Aaliyah. Preschool B's teacher was also deaf, however, she didn't use her voice and only signed. This was her first teaching assignment. Now I realize that all professionals have to start some place but for a group of children already lagging behind their hearing counterparts in development I didn't think that this was an appropriate first assignment. Both programs were Total Communication in which ASL was used as the sign system. Since preschool children are such conceptual learners, ASL is usually used more often than Signing Exact English. For example, if you were to read the sentence "The cat ran after the mouse." Conceptually, you would sign, "Cat chased mouse". Signing, "chase" would paint a clearer picture than signing, "ran after."

Each program had self-contained classrooms in which the classes only had deaf and hard of hearing children until grade 5. However, toward the later grades the children were mainstreamed into hearing classes if the children were ready for this move. When the child went to a mainstreamed class a sign language interpreter would be in those classes. I really believe that mainstreaming shouldn't be done until later elementary years. The focus of early elementary years should be on learning what is being taught straight from the teacher and not trying to adjust to what is being said in the classroom by the teacher through the interpreter.

Speech therapy and audiological services were other factors I considered when looking at both programs. Aaliyah would require extensive speech therapy and with her hearing aids I wanted an Audiologist available to examine her equipment and make sure that they were functioning properly at school. Preschool A's district had an Audiologist who made routine checks to the schools within the district that had children with assistive devices such as hearing aids. She would make ear molds when needed and would do hearing tests at the district's office. Preschool B contracted out to an Audiologist, which meant that the children had to leave the building to go to the Audiologist's clinic if anything went wrong with their aids. I preferred the idea of having the Audiologist come to the school. Both schools had speech therapists on site that had been working at each school for a number of years. Matter of fact, the speech therapist at Preschool B had once worked at Preschool A years before Aaliyah started. The director of the Deaf and Hard of Hearing program for Preschool B's district told me the program was not as strong in the speech and auditory training as Preschool A's program.

Lastly, I compared the physical layout and building condition of both schools. I didn't want Aaliyah to go to a run down school with potential hazards for her health or safety. Preschool A was an older building but well maintained. The school consisted of two buildings that were both one story. The Deaf and Hard of Hearing preschool through second grade class were held in a round building. The third through fifth grade classes were held in the main building with the hearing students. There was overhead covering attached from the round building to the main building. The playground area as well as the play equipment looked well taken care of. The cafeteria was a nice size and all the children ate together. I really liked the idea that all the children had a chance to interact with each other as children and not as the deaf students and the hearing students.

Yuck! was the best word I could use to explain Preschool B's building. It was dark and very dismal inside with poor lighting. I don't know if the building was older than Preschool A but it definitely looked older. Also, the children in the Deaf and Hard of Hearing program ate in their classrooms because "there were not enough tables in the cafeteria for the deaf students". Although I would like to say that I looked at both programs without prejudice, I can't. As I mentioned earlier I had already decided on Preschool A, but I felt better knowing that I went to Preschool B and looked at their program. Now, I knew I made the right decision and I informed the Parent Infant Specialist of it.

Just prior to completing the Parent Infant Program I had gone to the school district that we lived in and asked if Aaliyah could be released to the district Preschool A was in. I got the run around and I was told "Sure, we will let her go out of district if the other district will accept her." Well the other district said "Sure, we will take her if the other district lets her go." This conversational tennis match went on for a few weeks. I really didn't think that my choices would be limited to where we lived. Perhaps, my logic was a little off, but I thought surely districts would not restrict where I would like to send my deaf daughter considering my choices were already limited.

Finally, the day arrived when we were to go to the school to discuss Aaliyah's Individualized Education Program (IEP). An IEP is a written commitment of services that the school specifically designs to meet a child's special needs. Every child who goes to a public school and receives special education must have an IEP in effect before receiving these services. The purpose of the IEP is to establish learning goals for the child and to state the services that the school district will provide for the child. An IEP must be reviewed and revised at least annually, however, parents and/or the school may request a meeting more often than once per year.

The coordinator for the Deaf and Hard of Hearing Program from Preschool B informed us that their program was adequate for Aaliyah and that they would not release her to Preschool A. I was crushed. How could they play such a game with my child's education? How dare they tell me what is best for my daughter's education. Well, I learned from our day care provider at the time that a few of the children that attended the day care used that address to remain in that district. I was relieved to know that there was something I could do and I did it. We changed our address on all of the school forms to reflect our day care provider's address. I then notified Preschool B's district of this change and that Aaliyah would be attending Preschool A. I informed the Parent Infant Specialist of our choice and she wrote up Aaliyah's IEP which would then carry over to the fall. Aaliyah had her first IEP meeting on May 12, 1998 and she completed the Parent Infant Program on June 11th.

Aaliyah's first day of preschool was approaching quickly and I wanted to make sure that she was ready. I monitored the local paper religiously for back to school sales and when the perfect sale came I participated in the ritual that all parents look forward to. However, along with making sure she had new school clothes and supplies I wanted to make sure that her hearing aids were working properly so Aaliyah had an audiogram done before school started. The Audiologist's evaluation reported the following "Today's results indicated aided responses in the severe hearing loss range. The present hearing aids have a frequency response of 210-

5000 Hz. Hearing aids that have a further low frequency emphasis, the Oticon 390 PL aid, ranging from 75-4800 Hz may be of benefit to Aaliyah. Full-time use of amplification may also improve Aaliyah's awareness to sound. A FM System may be of benefit as well." FM Systems are designed to broadcast the speaker's voice directly to the ears of the individual listener. The teacher wears a compact microphone and transmitter while Aaliyah wears a receiver and earphones, which are attached to the bottom portion of the hearing aids, to hear the teacher clearly even from the back of the classroom.

After the results of the audiogram, I took the recommendations of the school audiologist to Aaliyah's military ENT physician and a few weeks later we received a new set of hearing aids as well as a FM System, which the military paid for. I wanted to make sure that Aaliyah started school with the best type of amplification.

In the fall of 1998, Aaliyah's first day of preschool had arrived. I was not ready for my baby to go to school but I knew it had to be done. Questions began running through my mind. Would an all day program be too much for her? When meeting other parents, would I feel guilty talking about my child being in school all day while their children were at home with them? I had to reassure myself that this was the right thing to do because she needed this type of environment that was structured and full of language in order for her to be as successful in the educational setting as her hearing peers.

Although I was nervous, I felt comfortable sending Aaliyah to Preschool A. Her class had a teacher and two assistants. Two of the three women were deaf all if not most of their lives. They were the only deaf people Aaliyah interacted with on a daily basis, which was very important to me. The other assistant was a certified sign language interpreter whose stepson was deaf. I felt that the relationship that would develop with these women would be a great introduction to the Deaf culture. They would show Aaliyah that being Deaf was not a disability but just a way of life. I looked at this as just one more way of putting a positive spin to God's challenges he brings us. As parents we are our children's most important role models and even though I can't share with Aaliyah the experience of being deaf, I can make sure that I fill her life with Deaf role models. It just worked out that these individuals were her teachers who eventually became family friends.

The drive to school seemed very fast even though it was a 35 minute drive. Once we arrived at school, I sat for a few moments in the car and watched as the teachers welcomed the children as they got off the bus and directed them to the appropriate class. It really bothered me to see these three-year-old children coming off of the bus. Where were their parents? Although the bus stopped directly in front of each child's home to pick him or her up, a 10 minute car ride took 30 minutes or longer by bus. I was not ready for Aaliyah to ride the bus and she was the only one that didn't. I drove her to and from that school until she was in the third grade. As I walked Aaliyah from the car to the round building where her classroom was, I held her hand tightly. I was so impressed that her face didn't show any signs of hesitation. She had a big bright smile on her face as she had every morning and her eyes were wide open with anticipation. When we entered the classroom, I gave her a giant kiss and hug. I told her that I loved her and that I would see her later. No sooner than I got the word "later" out, she was off playing with her friends. My baby was growing up and I may have cried a bit that day but I survived.

Aaliyah's preschool days were full of learning. The children worked on the alphabet, numbers, calendar time, story time, speech therapy, auditory training, lunch, naptime, snack time and other activities. I know I may come across as biased but Aaliyah was one of the best students in the class. (Well, at least I didn't say that she was THE best student in the class). She mastered the assignments without a lot of problem and she was definitely following in her big sister's footsteps of being a great student.

Along with doing well in preschool Aaliyah finally began to wear her hearing aids more consistently, eight hours a day five days a week however, wearing the FM was another story. Initially, there was always something wrong with the FM system but after a couple of months of repairs, Aaliyah was consistently wearing the FM as well. The use of both the hearing aids and FM system gave the teacher and I a better assessment of how well all of these amplification devices were really helping Aaliyah. Well, the answer was that they were not helping. The teacher and speech therapist reported that Aaliyah was not showing consistent responses to sounds and not doing well at auditory training considering she had hearing aids and a FM system.

It was time for another audiogram since it had been one year since the last one. The Audiologist's evaluation indicated the following "Aided responses were in the moderate to moderately severe hearing loss range at 125-250 Hz. The aided speech reception threshold was also in the moderate hearing loss range, which was an improvement of 25 dB from the previous evaluation of March 1998. Full time use of her hearing aids and the FM system, along with auditory training may further enhance the development of auditory skills." I was encouraged to see that her hearing loss classification was upgraded from severe to moderately severe when she wore her hearing aids. What did this mean? To the teachers and I it meant that Aaliyah should have responded to sounds that fell within her range on a more consistent basis while wearing her hearing aids and FM system.

With this in mind the teacher worked with Aaliyah for 10 minutes a day on auditory training. She really enjoyed doing this and worked hard to do her best. She began to show some understanding of when to respond to sounds by putting blocks into a can. She was able to hear loud “hooting” sounds but not a shout or her name yet. At first she was using her hearing aids only for auditory training and then began using the FM system also. The training consisted of practicing to respond to sounds such as a drum, bell, clapper, loud voice while hooting and normal voice while saying her name and colors. Usually Aaliyah consistently responded to sounds on the average of one time out of five attempts. Aaliyah’s awareness of sounds progressed very slowly. I felt guilty in some way because we were making her wear all this stuff and it really was not providing much amplification.

I can’t express in words how proud I was (and continue to be) of Aaliyah. She has always remained strong and very patient with us as we tried different amplification products. She never resisted wearing her hearing aids and FM system at school. At home the equipment usually came off but I didn’t push the issue because I didn’t want her to hate wearing her hearing aids. It became our routine in the morning to put the hearing aids and FM system on and when she came home from school or on weekends the hearing aids usually came off and stayed off. I think that Aaliyah wore her aids at school without resistance because the other children in the class and the teacher wore hearing aids. She was actually the only child in the class that had her own personnel FM system. The school had some older FM models but none of the other children wore them. The plan was to eventually get new FM systems for them to use at school.

Preschool was truly a wonderful experience. I felt that I had made a good decision in starting Aaliyah at this school because I could see her growth and development flourish in the school environment as well as home. How could it not? She had wonderful teachers and received a lot of love at home. Her environment was full of sign language. The communication channels between us were wide open with no obstructions. She was happy, loving, and wonderful to be with. When I would walk her to her class many of her friends would run to greet her in the morning excited that she was there. When I would pick her up from school, sometimes I would arrive a few minutes early just so I could watch her play with her friends on the playground. She never played favorites and seemed to play with all the children, even the ones that the other children may not have liked as much. It was exhilarating to see how much passion she had for life interacting with others and not letting her lack of hearing get in the way. Aaliyah's teachers became my friends and I enjoyed interacting with each of them and learning about the Deaf culture.

The end of the preschool years was a real eye opener for me. I realized that even with hearing aids and the FM system Aaliyah was not hearing very well. I started to question the necessity of the hearing aids. Would I be doing the right thing by not having her wear the hearing aids? Was it fair to have her continue wearing the aids even though she was not getting a great deal of benefit from them? Was there something different out there that I should be considering such as a cochlear implant?

Aaliyah on a school field trip to the zoo

Chapter 9

Sign Language Interpreters

Along with the parent, teacher, speech therapist, and audiologist another essential person in the life of a deaf child who communicates with sign language is a sign language interpreter. An interpreter is a professional that serves as a communication link between the deaf and the hearing person using sign language. When deaf individuals want to listen to or speak with someone who does not know sign language, or visa versa, they use a sign language interpreter. To be a successful communication link, the interpreter must relay the meaning of a message as accurately as possible.

Interpreters are utilized in the educational, medical, legal, recreational, mental health, religious, personal, financial, vocational, and any other setting where the deaf and hearing need to communicate with each other. Some settings we have used interpreters included the classroom, our home, church, doctor appointments, after-school programs, tee ball, ballet classes, gymnastics, and a Disney on Ice show.

The Americans with Disabilities Act (ADA) is a law that prohibits discrimination against people who are deaf and hearing impaired as well as others with disabilities. The ADA expects agencies, businesses, service providers, and employers to be accessible to the deaf and hearing impaired by furnishing auxiliary aids and services, which are necessary to ensure effective communication. Qualified interpreters are one example of an auxiliary aid and service outlined in the ADA. A qualified interpreter is defined as an interpreter who is able to sign to the individual who is deaf what is being said by the hearing person and who can voice to the hearing person what is being signed by the individual who is deaf. This communication must be conveyed effectively, accurately, and impartially, through the use of any necessary specialized vocabulary.

Title II of the ADA requires that all types of state and local government agencies and entities provide effective communication to deaf and hearing - impaired individuals. Examples of agencies and entities that fall under this title include courts, schools, social service agencies, jails, police and fire departments, legislatures, commissions and councils, municipal golf courses, civic arenas and lottery bureaus.

Title III of the ADA covers businesses and nonprofit service providers that are public accommodations, privately operated entities offering certain types of courses and examinations, privately operated transportation, and commercial facilities. Public accommodations are private entities that own, lease, lease to, or operate facilities. Examples of public accommodations that must provide effective communication to deaf and hearing-impaired individuals include:

-Places of lodging (inns, hotels, motels)
-Establishments serving food or drink (restaurants and bars)
-Places of exhibition or entertainment (movie theaters, concert halls, stadiums)
-Sales or rental establishments (bakeries, grocery stores, hardware stores, shopping centers)
-Service establishments (Laundromats, dry-cleaners, banks, barbershops, beauty shops, travel services, funeral parlors, gas stations, offices of accountants or lawyers, pharmacies, insurance offices, hospitals, and offices of health care providers)
-Places with public transportation terminals, depots, or stations (not including facilities relating to air transportation).
-Places of public display or collection (museums, libraries, galleries).
-Places of recreation (parks, zoos, amusement parks)
-Places of education (nursery schools, elementary, secondary, undergraduate, or post-graduate private schools)
-Places of exercise or recreation (gymnasiums, health spas, bowling alleys, golf courses).
-Social service center establishments (day care centers, senior citizen centers, homeless shelters, food banks, adoption agencies)
-Privately run child care centers - like other public accommodations must comply with title III of the Americans with Disabilities Act and provide appropriate auxiliary aids such as interpreters and services needed for effective communication.

A public accommodation cannot use a staff member who signs "pretty well" as an interpreter for meetings because signing and interpreting is not the same thing. Being able to sign does not mean that a person can process spoken communication into the proper signs, nor does it mean that he or she possesses the proper skills to observe someone signing and change their signed or finger spelled communication into spoken words. Also, the signer's attitudes or emotions could affect the objectivity and impartiality needed to provide accurate communication. The interpreter must be able to interpret both receptively and expressively.

If a sign language interpreter is required for effective communication, must only a certified interpreter be provided? No. The key question in determining whether effective communication will result is whether the interpreter is "qualified," not whether he or she has been actually certified by an official licensing body. A qualified interpreter is one "who is able to interpret effectively, accurately and impartially, both receptively and expressively, using any necessary specialized vocabulary." An individual does not have to be certified in order to meet this standard.

A certified interpreter must pass an exam that may be written or oral. The interpreter education program covers a variety of areas including the role of an interpreter, a historical overview of the interpreting profession, public speaking techniques, understanding of and sensitivity to the deaf community, linguistics and language development. The program also covers the interpreter's code of ethics, physical factors involved in interpreting, the various specialized situations in which an interpreter might function, and extensive guided practice in the skills involved in interpreting. Once the program has been completed and the examination has been passed the interpreter is awarded a certification based on level of competency by a national professional organization such as the Registry of Interpreters for the Deaf, Inc. and the National Association of the Deaf. Interpreters then can decide to get into even more specific areas of interpreting including legal, medical/mental health, educational and tactile interpreting (interpreting for deaf-blind individuals).

We have always had certified interpreters for Aaliyah in the medical, educational, and church settings. However, for events such as tee ball, gymnastics, ballet, and after-school programs obtaining a certified interpreter is much more difficult. It all comes down to the almighty dollar. Businesses that we have dealt with were always receptive to having an interpreter on-site if they didn't have to pay for them. However, if we were assertive with our request we were the recipient of the catch phrase "it would be an undue financial burden" in order to scare us from pursuing the request. Although the ADA is a law and should be black and white in its meaning, it does give businesses an out by stating that if the accommodation would cause an "undue financial burden" than they do not have to provide the accommodation. Well, if that's the case one would think that all businesses would claim financial hardship when making accommodations. However, if a parent is willing to go the extra mile and file a complaint or take legal action, then the organization will have to prove that indeed providing an interpreter would be detrimental to their business.

Aaliyah and other deaf children should be provided effective communication that would allow the same participation as hearing children. As parents it is our responsibility to know all the laws that enable this equality to take place. I have really learned a lot as I grow in my assertiveness to be Aaliyah's advocate. If we don't hold society and it's businesses accountable to provide equal access to all individuals then the struggles of all those individuals who have been treated with inequality have been for naught. In essence, we would be allowing society to place our children in mental prisons because their aspirations would be unobtainable. I want Aaliyah to know that I have worked hard to help remove the barriers that would prevent her from participating in whatever she chose to be involved in. One organization I did do battle with regarding interpreting services was Disney. That's right! Mickey Mouse himself.

On March 28, 2001, I went to a travel agency that specialized in cruise vacation packages. I expressed my interest in arranging a Disney vacation package and was given a number of different package options. I decided on the 4-night Walt Disney World stay followed by a 3-night Disney cruise. I informed the travel agent that we would need a sign language interpreter for Aaliyah while on the cruise ship for the children activities and show. I told him that if our request for an interpreter was not met that we would not go on the cruise. The travel agent said, "Disney is very accommodating to those with disabilities" as he pointed to the page in the Disney brochure that highlighted a section titled Guests with Disabilities. The brochure stated "If you would like to request accommodations for guests with disabilities, please advise the reservationists of any special needs at the time of booking." The travel agent filled out a cruise price proposal sheet, which listed the total cost of the vacation package and told me that Disney required a deposit to confirm our reservation.

A few days after talking with the travel agent we made our initial deposit and was informed by Disney to call closer to the sail date to make sure an interpreter would be available for the sail date of 1/13/02. During the week of Sep 17, 2001, the travel agent called me to let me know that Disney would have an interpreter on board for our sail date but only for the evening shows and lifeboat drills. A few days later I called Disney's Medical Special Service Coordinator for clarification on the role of the interpreter since she was the one responsible for making the arrangements. She told me the interpreters' contract stated that they only interpret the Disney shows and the lifeboat drills. I was frustrated to hear that since the interpreters were already on the cruise ship they would not interpret the children's activities during the day even though they were available for the shows in the evening. They were already on the cruise ship. The Medical Special Service Coordinator stated that she understood my plight but continued to offer no compromise or meet any part of my request. She said the interpreters' contract was up for negotiation at the time and would be finalized in October. In the mean time she didn't know what the negotiations entailed and therefore could not say what they would or would not be able to interpret in January. She stated that Disney followed ADA guidelines strictly and even went beyond what is expected of them.

Yes. Disney was most accommodating in providing a TTY and signal lights for the stateroom we were going to be in. However, these were not appropriate assistive devices for Aaliyah who was six at the time. Who was she going to call and when would we leave her alone in the room without us? At one point during my interaction with the Medical Special Service Coordinator, she suggested that perhaps the counselors on board could draw pictures and write instructions down for Aaliyah. Hello, she was six years old and just beginning to read, I doubt this would be an effective way to communicate instructions.

On Sep 27, 2001, I mailed an ADA complaint letter to the Department of Justice. I was told that this process could take a few months since the Department of Justice priorities were focused on catching terrorists following September 11th. A few days after mailing the ADA complaint, we canceled our vacation and got all of our money back. I was furious and we were all very disappointed. Aaliyah asked me "Why won't the man let me on the mouse ship?" How could Disney do this? I sent a letter to the Chairman of Walt Disney Parks and Resorts hoping they would take the opportunity to fix the situation. In the letter I stated "I am very saddened and disappointed with Disney's lack of sensitivity in meeting the needs of my deaf daughter. My daughter has been discriminated against because she is deaf. We were initially very impressed with the product of the Disney World/Disney Cruise package because we thought that this would be an ideal family vacation. This would have been our first real vacation since the birth of my daughter. We thought this experience would be one that we would remember for a lifetime and heard great things about the cruise. What really sold us on this package was the amount of activities that were available for the children on board the cruise ship".

I went on to explain the events leading up to our cancellation and asked Disney to provide us with the interpreting services that we initially requested. I thought I would try to appeal to their sense of decency and asked that they not disappoint Aaliyah a second time by not giving her the opportunity to build childhood memories or allowing their corporation's name to be used in the same sentence as discrimination.

On November 14, 2001, I received the following letter from Disney in response to the letter I had sent them. Please note that in the letter it does not say anything about the interpreters being available for the children's activities.

Dear Mrs. Cheatham:

Thank you for writing to Paul Pressler concerning your experiences booking with Disney Cruise Line. As you can imagine, Paul receives a large amount of mail each day. Although he is very concerned about our guests, he has asked me to respond on his behalf, and I welcome the opportunity to do so.

First and foremost, I hope you will accept my sincere regret for any disappointment with the complimentary interpretation services that we offer our guests with hearing disabilities onboard our cruise ships. I can assure you that serving the needs of all our guests, including those with disabilities, is very important to us. The Disney organization has been an industry leader in provisions for guests with disabilities on land and at sea; great enhancements are continually being made to provide an enjoyable vacation for everyone.

As you know, American Sign Language interpreters are available to provide complimentary interpretation for live performances on designated cruise dates throughout the year. We can also equip any stateroom with Communication Kits, which are available upon request and based upon availability. These kits include a base unit with an alarm clock, bed shaker notification, doorknocker and telephone alerts, a strobe light smoke detector, and a TTY. All televisions onboard our cruise ships are equipped with closed captioning capabilities. Furthermore, we offer Assistive Listening Devices, which uses infrared signals to amplify audio for live performances and other shows, as well as Guest Assistance Packets that contain show scripts, flashlight, pen, and paper, which can be signed-out and kept until the night before disembarkation. We truly want all of our guests to have fond memories of their time spent with Disney, and we are very proud of the reputation we have achieved in terms of family entertainment and guest service. We appreciate your observations and suggestions and will certainly take them into consideration.

I would also like to mention that with Disney's Oceaneer Club our counselors are happy to help where they can, however, we are unable to provide one-on-one care for your daughter in our children's programming. A parent or caregiver must accompany any child who has special needs requiring one-on-one attention. You may be interested to know that we offer a special $75.00 per day rate for any caregiver a parent may bring aboard for a child with special needs, such as your daughter. Further information regarding this special rate is available by calling our Special Services Coordinator at 1-800-511-1333 and asking for extension 67735.

Again, I truly am sorry for any disappointment and hope that this will not affect your regard for Disney Cruise Line. We would truly appreciate the opportunity to welcome you and your family aboard one of our cruise ships in the near future.

Sincerely,
George Parker, Manager of Guest Communications

In December, I called the Medical Special Service Coordinator once again to see if anything had changed with the interpreters' contract and nothing had. One week later I called the Guest Communications office (the same office that sent me the letter) because I was not giving up. I thought if anything they would get tired of me calling and finally let us go on the cruise with the interpreting services we had requested. An individual in that office said that Disney did not provide baby-sitting service.

The nerve of Disney! I never asked for a baby-sitter for Aaliyah. But let us take a closer look at the definition. According to Webster's Dictionary a baby-sitter is a person hired to care for one or more children when the parents are away. On the Disney Cruise Line there are "counselors" in charge of the children during the children's activities as parents are given pagers so they can leave their children while they attend other activities. It looks like the counselors are "baby-sitters" according to the dictionary. I guess for the Smith family, whose child or children do not have a disability the children are being watched by counselors and for the Cheatham family the person watching Aaliyah would be called a baby-sitter. A little discriminatory don't you think. Oh yes, apparently Disney thought they were being gracious by informing me that I could be Aaliyah's interpreter for a caregiver rate of $75.00/day. How nice of them! Our family vacation now has turned into a job for me.

In January of 2002, five months after sending my ADA complaint, I received a letter from the Department of Justice. The following is an excerpt from the letter. "After a review of the matter you have raised, we have decided not to take any further action. Our decision does not indicate whether or not we believe there has been a violation of the ADA in this instance. Nor does our decision affect your rights, as an affected individual, to seek correction of the problems you have identified. You are free to file a private suite in Federal Court."

After I canceled our vacation, I began to see numerous commercials on TV advertising Disney's 100th year celebration. Disney should have changed their commercials to "Come celebrate our 100th year anniversary with your family but if you have a deaf child stay home." Disney's discrimination against Aaliyah was not right and I wanted to do something about this. I began searching for an attorney who specialized in ADA issues and would be willing to take on this case. I contacted the National Association of the Deaf (NAD) since they had filed a lawsuit against Walt Disney World in the past and the matter was resolved. NAD informed me that they often CO-counsel with other attorneys on a variety of cases and to have our attorney contact them. However, we didn't have an attorney and it was very difficult finding one who specialized in ADA issues and had reasonable fees. I guess I was hoping to find an attorney who would take this case on a contingency basis, which meant that they got paid if they won the case. I must have called and emailed at least 30 attorneys locally as well as in Florida. Most of the attorneys listed as specializing in ADA issues, dealt with employment issues. Some were not sure about the jurisdiction involved with the case. Local attorneys told me to contact Florida attorneys since that is where the Cruise ship's port was and some Florida attorneys told me that local attorneys could take the case because

Disney provides their product nationally. Others were asking for fees anywhere from $5,000 to $10,000. One local attorney told me "Wouldn't you rather use that money for a different type of vacation".

I had searched for six months and just when I was ready to give up, I decided to perform one last search on the Internet related to lawsuits and cruise lines. I contacted a law firm in Florida who had filed lawsuits against other cruise lines. An attorney from that office referred me to another attorney who had specifically sued the Disney Cruise Line before. His name was Matthew Dietz and he was located in Miami, Florida. But before I hung up, I asked her how realistic was my expectation to find an attorney to take this case on a contingency basis. She told me that most ADA attorneys take their cases on a contingency basis and that gave me the affirmation I needed to call Mr. Dietz.

After my initial conversation with Mr. Dietz, I felt that he would be the attorney to help us win our complaint against Disney. He definitely had the background for dealing with Disney's attorney as well as understanding their tactics. He shared with me that he was frustrated with Disney's practices against the disabled and expressed a huge sense of motivation in making sure that he was going to do all he could to get Disney to resolve this matter. He informed me that he would take this case on a contingency basis and would be putting a lot of work and hours into this case. He expected the same commitment from me, which would not be hard to do since my commitment already became vested six months earlier.

The day after our initial conversation, I sent Mr. Dietz all the written information I had which explained in detail what happened. I kept a detailed log of the people I spoke with, when I spoke with them and what they said. I also, kept much of my conversations with Disney via email or writing so that I had proof of what was said. It wasn't long after this that I received a letter from Mr. Dietz stating that he had received the information and enclosed a copy of a letter that he wrote to Disney's attorney. In his letter he stated if "Magical (Disney cruises) refuses to provide a sign language interpreter, then we can push forward and file our complaint with the Florida Commission, wait 180 days, until they make a finding, and then file suit pursuant to the Act and the ADA."

The following is a few of the paragraphs that were contained in the letter to Disney's attorney. "To recap our discussion, Aaliyah is a six-year old who is deaf. Her mother would like to take her on a Disney Cruise, but Disney refuses to use its sign language interpreters to interpret other services and programs offered to Aaliyah, so she could enjoy her cruise as would any other six-year old. What especially troubles me is the letter dated November 14, 2001. The term "complimentary interpretation services" is misleading, and imposing an inordinate surcharge of hiring a caregiver on a cruise and/or requiring parental supervision blatantly violates the American with Disabilities Act."

"It is reasonable to assume that providing Aaliyah with an interpreter would not be a fundamental alteration to the services offered by Magical Cruises. Nor would it be an undue burden on Magical to provide Aaliyah an interpreter so she (and her parents) could benefit from the accommodations provided for their fare."

"If you refuse to make a reasonable modification in policies and procedures for Aaliyah and her parents, we will file a complaint with the Florida Commission on Human Rights for damages under 509.092, and additionally, file suit pursuant to Title III of the Americans with Disabilities Act. Please advise the undersigned of Magical Cruises intention within the next 21 days from the date of this letter."

Roughly, one week after sending this letter, Disney's attorney contacted our attorney, and afterwards he called me to give me an update. Apparently Disney's attorney had said something to the affect "What would you like us to do, have someone walk around with Aaliyah on the ship all day." Also, Disney's attorney had made a comment that at age six, he could read (I am sure implying that Aaliyah should also be reading at that age) and that if Disney provided transcripts for her then she should be able to read those. That attorney was certainly gifted if he could read transcripts at the age of six.

On April 30, 2002, Disney's attorney had requested two more weeks before giving us an answer because apparently, the individual who would be making the decision was in Japan setting up Disney Land. Two weeks later, on May 17th, Disney's attorney once again asked for two more weeks to do additional research on this issue to determine if other cruise lines provided interpreters. Although my attorney and I felt that Disney was stone walling us we decided to give Disney two more weeks before filing our official complaint. Also, in the event that this matter did get resolved, we required Magical to publish the availability of interpreters for the deaf and otherwise hearing impaired for all of its programs on Magical's vessels, so this situation would not be repeated with Aaliyah or any other child in the future. If Disney did not agree to this then we would file an administrative complaint, which meant that we would file for damages under the Florida Human Rights Commission and for policy changes under the Title III of the ADA.

On June 10th, Mr. Dietz called and asked for my permission to let the attorneys from NAD be CO-Counsel. He explained that it would be beneficial to our side to have a national association backing us and of course, I said that would be fine. A few days later I received a copy of a letter that our attorney sent to NAD in which he enclosed the proposed complaint to the Florida Commission on Human Relation. Also, in his letter he pointed out to NAD that there were no reported cases of this type related to failing to provide a person with a sign-language interpreter under Florida State law. Our case would be the first for the state. The following day Mr. Dietz received the following letter from Disney's counsel.

> Dear Matt:
>
> I am responding to your correspondence dated April 8, 2002 in connection with the above referenced matter on behalf of Magical Cruise Company, Limited d/b/a Disney Cruise Line. I wanted to assure you and your client that Disney Cruise Line values and appreciates all of its guests and welcomes any comments that might improve the quality of the services offered. As you are aware, Disney Cruise Line prides itself as being a service and guest oriented company. Nevertheless, as we have discussed in our telephone conversations, Disney Cruise Line must respectfully disagree that it has violated any applicable laws or regulations with respect to its guest with disabilities.
>
> The assertions contained in your letter appear to be based upon a misunderstanding of Disney Cruise Line's services. Contrary to Ms. Cheatham's claims, Disney Cruise Line provides interpreters for many of its onboard programs including, but not limited to live theater shows, life boat drills, and various other onboard activities and programs upon request, such as Tea with Wendy Darling, debarkation talk, shopping and shore excursion talks, dueling pianos, variety acts, wine tasting, dining experiences and other shipboard classes and presentations.
>
> Disney Cruise Line strives to provide excellent services to all of its guests, including those with disabilities. In an effort to continually improve the services it provides, Disney Cruise Line also makes available sign language interpreters, on an as-available basis for selected children's programming in order to interpret instructions necessary for participation. That means that interpreters will be provided to interpret instructions and other information for children's programming activities on Dis-

ney Cruise Line's scheduled interpreted cruises on a request basis, subject to availability and lack of conflict with regularly scheduled interpreted programs (i.e., live theater shows).

Your statements concerning Mr. Parker's response are not accurate and are taken out of context. Disney Cruise Line does provide complimentary interpretation services in those instances set forth above. Mr. Parker merely indicated that Disney does not provide one-on-one, twenty-four hour, interpretive services since such services would amount to a caregiver status.

As you know, in connection with any request to provide interpreters, a public accommodation is not required to provide individuals with disabilities with services of a personal nature. Furthermore, a public accommodation is only obligated to provide effective communication and is not obligated to undertake an undue burden. The services provided by Disney Cruise Line comply with all obligations under the applicable disability laws.

We trust that the foregoing addresses the issues raised in your letter. Please do not hesitate to contact me if you wish to discuss this matter further.

Sincerely,
Greenberg, Traurig, P.A. / Brian C. Blair

Attached to this letter Disney provided a copy of the published policy on the availability of interpreters, which states the following. "Disney Cruise Line provides complimentary Sign Language interpretation for live theater performances and other shows and events on select sailings. Disney Cruise Line also makes available sign language interpreters, on an as-available basis for selected children's programming in order to interpret instructions necessary for participation. That means that interpreters will be provided to interpret instructions and other information for children's programming activities on Disney Cruise Line's scheduled interpreted cruises on a request basis, subject to availability and lack of conflict with regularly scheduled interpreted programs (i.e., live theater shows). Guests can request sailing dates and other information by calling Disney Cruise Line Information at (407) 566-3500 (voice) or (407) 566 7455 (TTY). Reservations must be confirmed 60 days prior to departure to ensure interpretation availability. While onboard, please contact Guest services for further information about or to request Sign Language interpretation services."

A few weeks later, Mr. Dietz contacted me to let me know what he and the attorneys for NAD had discussed. It was suggested that it would be a much stronger case for us if we could find a family with a deaf child who had already gone on the Disney Cruise and had been denied interpreting services. Since Disney did publish their policy regarding their interpreting services we won that part of the battle. However, it was explained to me that we would not be able to argue discrimination unless we actually went on the cruise. Disney's stance was that if we had gone on the Cruise, we wouldn't have been discriminated against, and therefore would have no damages. Our attorney and NAD told me that this was a valid position but if we go on the cruise at a later date and are discriminated against then this may be viewed as continuing discrimination, despite the one-year limitations period under Florida law.

Since we were unsuccessful in locating a family, the next plan according to our attorney was to go on the cruise. I did go to a travel agent to begin the process again for us to go on the cruise. I wanted to see how easy it would be this time and if the employees knew Disney's policy. Interestingly, there were still some inconsistencies amongst Disney personnel as to who was aware and unaware of the published policy dated 07/01.

In July of 2002, I had gone to a travel agency to look into booking another Disney vacation package. The travel agent spoke with a Disney customer service representative as I sat on the other side of the agent's desk. She told me that an interpreter would be available for the children's activities on selected dates. I was happy to see that Disney was following their policy. However, I was still troubled by the restrictions placed on the actual sail dates. I was given sail dates for 2002 and 2003 which were not convenient for family's with school age children.

A day later, I called Disney customer service myself to get more information on dates. This time I spoke with "Candace" who didn't know about Disney's interpreter's policy. She spoke with her supervisor and then told me that the interpreter WOULD NOT be available for the children's activities during the day and would only be available for the shows and any public event open to all adults and children. When I explained to her that this was different information I had received the day before, she told me that I was misinformed. Now I was getting frustrated because let us not forget Disney had published their policy which employees should have been aware of.

I thought that if I had gotten such different responses one day apart, what type of response would I get calling later in the same day. Well, later that day, I spoke with "Rich" who quickly found Disney's policy regarding sign language interpreters. A few days after speaking with “Rich”, I called Disney again and spoke with "Lee". She talked with her supervisor because she never had this question asked before and like "Candace" was unaware of the policy. After speaking with her supervisor, she told me that priority for the interpreter on board the cruise ship was for the live performances so if Aaliyah wanted to participate in an activity while a performance was going on that she would not get the interpreter.

The day after I spoke with "Lee", I decided to call the Medical Service Coordinator once again. I wanted to see if this person was aware of the published policy since this would be the person making arrangements for interpreting services for Aaliyah. She said that Disney decided not to have specific sail dates because they found that in the past they had to cancel the interpreter because there were no hearing impaired people on those designated cruises or the cruises with hearing-impaired people had no interpreters available. As a result Disney waits to make sure that the reservation has been confirmed before a note is made to the Medical Service Coordinator to make arrangements for the interpreter. The Medical Service Coordinator stated that the interpreter would be available for the shows and the children's programs for instructional purposes. I was curious to know on the average how many hearing-impaired people are on the cruise and I was told usually 3-4 people, although one time they did have a large group on board.

Well, this whole situation has been a learning experience. I am happy that Disney published its policies regarding the availability of sign language interpreters. However, what good is a policy that your own employees are unaware of. All I can say is shame on Disney for not training their employees thoroughly and for disappointing my daughter. Companies should have disability sensitivity training, which would go over things such as interpreting services to make sure all employees are aware of this policy. Bravo to those attorneys such as Mr. Dietz and associations such as the National Association of the Deaf for standing up to corporations such as Disney protecting the rights of deaf individuals and individuals with disabilities.

I have come to the conclusion that giant corporations such as Disney as well as privately owned businesses are insensitive to the needs of deaf children requiring the service of an interpreter. Along with our battle with Disney, we also experienced resistance with our request for an interpreter with Aaliyah's gymnastic center she was attending once a week. This was a privately owned establishment, PSSG, which was opened to the public. When I first registered her, I asked for an interpreter and was told that they had not run into this request before and our conversation was left at that. I was told that I would be allowed on the floor to act as her interpreter even though parents were not allowed on the floor. This would allow me to closely observe how well the coaches worked with Aaliyah.

Five weeks had gone by and we both really liked the facility and the coaches. Aaliyah really enjoyed going to gymnastics but I was feeling a bit inadequate in the area of interpreting gymnastic signs so I had typed up a formal request for an interpreter. Enclosed with the letter, I included a list of the sign language interpreters in the area, sign language interpreting schools and information about a Web site that dealt with sign language interpreters for sports. I thought that this information would be useful in finding an interpreter whether they were a student going through training or an interpreter who was certified. Also, I gave PSSG information on how to obtain a packet containing information on how a small business can get a tax deduction to help offset some of the costs of improving accessibility for customers with disabilities.

Two weeks had gone by when the owner approached me during class regarding my request. Get your violins out for the following list of excuses. "The cheapest sign language interpreter I found was $40.00 per hour." "It would affect my business financially if I had to hire an interpreter." "I really don't make very much in this business." "The tax incentive information was not really worth it for this business." I know, I know the tears are flowing and get ready for the big suggestion which didn't include providing an interpreter "I was thinking about making flash cards with pictures on the different routines." Well, I was certainly blown away by this suggestion but I continued to interpret for Aaliyah while the coaches were working on these flash cards. One week later, I received a phone call from an attorney who works for PSSG and she wanted to reiterate that they wanted to help Aaliyah as much as they could.

The following Tuesday I found out that the attorney was actually one of the coaches as she came up to me with her white folder full of the information I had given the owner. Yet, again I had to pull out my violin. She began to tell me how she had known the owner for many, many, years and that "he is a wonderful person who tries to help everyone." She informed me that although legally he really didn't have to provide an interpreter he wanted to do the right thing. Are you gagging yet? She continued to say that PSSG lost money last year and the only other source of income for his family came from his wife who was a PHYSICIAN. Needless to say, this attorney was not winning my sympathy for this place or the owner. What really irritated me the most with our conversation was when she talked about a family friend who had a deaf son. Apparently, this mother had the financial resources to fly her son all over the world for the best surgeries and schools necessary for him and was very passionate about making sure he had everything he needed. I felt that she was telling me that if I was just as passionate about Aaliyah's needs than I would hire an interpreter for her and not expect PSSG to do this. This attorney was getting on my nerve and she was constantly calling our home with all these suggestions that involved us meeting the needs of PSSG and them not meeting Aaliyah's needs. One of her suggestions was to switch days when there were fewer children in the gym and therefore less noise. Another was to have Aaliyah wear her cochlear implant because they thought the she would be able to magically understand everything while wearing it and it would allow PSSG to escape meeting their obligation. A third suggestion was to make sure Aaliyah had the same coach all the time for consistency. As you can clearly see, PSSG threw out many suggestions so they would look good in the event that legal action were taken and then they could claim that we did not take them up on any of their suggestions. Did you notice that not one of the suggestions mentioned providing an interpreter. I continued to interpret while PSSG continued to offer stupid suggestions and I tolerated this situation because Aaliyah really enjoyed gymnastics. Yes, I could have sought legal advice regarding this but I didn't want to pursue a lawsuit every time our request for an interpreter was denied.

Well, in 2004 the time did come. I sought legal advice against another gymnastic center. I couldn't let this slide like I did the first go around. If I did than I wouldn't be a good advocate for Aaliyah because she would never be able to exceed in her talents as long as her main mode of communication was sign language.

After she finished her first year at Northshore Gymnastic Center (NGC), the coach recommended that Aaliyah move up to the next level in the fall because she had been doing so well. This level involved competitions. The coach reassured me that she would be Aaliyah's coach again and was planning to take sign language classes during the summer. I agreed with her recommendations however the classes were going to be held twice a week. This meant that I would only be able to attend the last part of the session. My brain went into first gear trying to come up with a solution to this dilemma.

One thing I knew I needed to do was request that the center provide an interpreter. This had to be made in writing because I wanted a paper trial in case I was met with resistance. In addition to making this request, I wanted to show the center that I really wanted this to be a collaborative approach in working towards a solution that would be beneficial to both Aaliyah and the center's pocket book. Providing the previous center with an abundance of information regarding the ADA and contact information for interpreters and agencies was not effective. I had to come up with another plan. Where would I find an interpreter that was inexpensive? Free would be even better. After much thinking I realized that a volunteer would be perfect. Except, where would I find one. I was not a member of a church with potential volunteers nor did I belong to any organizations. Then one day while I was commuting home from work, I passed a freeway exit sign with the name of a community college. Of course, that was it! I needed to contact the colleges with Sign Language Interpreter Training Programs. Perhaps the students would be interested in volunteering. I found that there were two programs in my state and I emailed the director of both programs explaining my situation and asking them to pass the information on to their students. As I waited for a response from the college, I wrote and faxed my request for an interpreter to the gymnastic center.

In the letter I clearly explained my request for an interpreter and the requirements by the ADA law to provide effective communication. I also mentioned that I was working on a solution as well. Since the coach felt that Aaliyah was good enough to move up to the next level and she represented the center I thought that they would be more willing to provide an interpreter than the previous gymnastic center we belonged to. I did not see how they could turn down our request. However, once again I was let down by the world of recreational sports and in particular gymnastics. A few days later I followed up with the center and spoke with the program coordinator who said that she was unclear as to what I was asking for. I swear that my letter was written in English so why it was unclear I will never understand. Since the college year had not started yet I began to send emails to professional interpreters asking if they would volunteer their services. I thought this would cover my bases between the certified interpreters and student interpreters. On August 18, 2004 I received this letter from the gymnastic center.

Dear Ms. Cheatham,

After talking to representatives of the Disability and Business Technical Assistance Center and the Department of Justice ADA Line, we have determined it would be an undue burden for our business to provide an interpreter for Aaliyah.

The language of gymnastics is specialized and to provide a qualified interpreter would be very difficult. With the hearing aid on, she can hear and understand the instructions given by a coach. The coaching style used in the class provides demonstration of skills as a way to communicate effectively with the gymnasts.

We would HIGHLY recommend the use of the hearing aid during the class it will allow her to have the most success in class since part of the curriculum is performing routines to music. We have contacted a hearing resources center to try to get some information on how to effectively attach the device to her head.

We are planning on providing these services to you as part of Aaliyah's participation in the program:

- We will give you a copy of all the routines Aaliyah is performing so that she can study them at home.
- We will post a copy of the routines at every event to help with communication.
- We will instruct the coach to demonstrate as much as possible or have another child demonstrate.
- We will instruct the coach to have Aaliyah stand close to her to facilitate giving her corrections in class at all the events.

We feel that this will provide an effective workout environment for Aaliyah.

Sincerely,
L.Y (Northshore Gymnastics Center)

Along with this letter, L.Y sent an email stating "We have been in contact with the ADA regarding our responsibility regarding Aaliyah. According to the 2 offices we contacted, they felt we are not under any obligation to provide an interpreter in this case. We have ways to communicate with her (as we have done the past year)."

YOU HAVE GOT TO BE KIDDING! All I ask is for my daughter to be given the same opportunity as the hearing children to learn how to perfect their technique in a sport. It broke my heart to see the coach and the other girls having conversations about the routines or maybe what they did at school that day but Aaliyah would just look around because she didn't understand what is being said. Oh sure, Aaliyah and the girls made casual gestures to each other by waving or smiling but she was only in their group, not really a part of their group.

For safety reasons I wanted someone who signed at the center in case Aaliyah got hurt and I was not there. It didn't make sense that a facility that promoted an environment that allowed children to grow in a skill and in their overall development expect me to dump my child off and have no one there to communicate to her.

The center's attitude forced me to investigate what recourse I could take. First I informed the center that since we had not resolved the interpreter issue I would keep Aaliyah in the same level as the previous year. I felt better knowing that I would be there for the entire class if she needed me to interpret or if she got injured. Second I asked Aaliyah's audiologist to write a letter highlighting the fact that a Cochlear Implant did not restore her hearing to normal as the center implied in their letter. The letter also listed concerns that we both shared if Aaliyah should wear her implant at gymnastics. Lastly, I contacted an attorney at the Washington Coalition of Citizens with disAbilities.

I had hoped that my letter from the audiologist and an attorney would let the center know that I meant business. I gave the attorney all my documented correspondence with the center and he went to work on my case. Prior to class starting we received a letter back from the center stating "I feel we have, and will continue to work on effective ways to communicate with Aaliyah without placing an undue burden on our program". In essence, the center said that they would not pay for an interpreter.

Classes began the first week of September and we still did not have an interpreter. We continued to wait for a volunteer to answer our call and we waited for the attorney to get us results. In February, six months after giving the attorney all my information and countless conversations with his assistant, I got a call from the attorney. His tone throughout the whole conversation lacked enthusiasm and basically led me to believe he didn't want to take this case although his assistant said otherwise. Right off the bat, he told me that although there was no precise formula in the law to calculate what is or is not an undue burden; he felt that it would be a financial burden for the center to provide an interpreter at a cost of $720.00 if I only paid $100.00 for a six week session.

He stated that he could write a letter to the center recommending more financially feasible alternatives. One alternative was finding a volunteer interpreter, which I had already been working on for months. The second alternative was splitting the cost of the interpreter, which in essence meant that I would pay more for gymnastics classes than the "smith" family. The third alternative, which I thought was a good idea as a last resort was videotaping the routines with an interpreter. At this point I was so fed up with his lack of enthusiasm and help I told him that I could handle things from here. Now here is the best part. He told me that if I wrote a letter to the center I should thank them for all they have done for Aaliyah (which was nothing) and allowing her to participate in their program (which I paid for her to participate in). Well, about two weeks later I received three phone calls from interpreter training program (ITP) students who offered to volunteer at gymnastics. This worked out great for Aaliyah because not only did she look forward to having the ITP student in her class but she also took the initiative to demonstrate certain routines when asked. We continued to get volunteer interpreters and they applied the hours they spent at gymnastics toward hours of community service for their degree. Unfortunately, just before moving to the next level Aaliyah began to have problems with her wrist on and off so she decided she wanted a break from gymnastics.

My experience in requesting for paid interpreters for recreational sports has and always will be met with resistance and that is a shame. I really believe that if Aaliyah (or any other deaf child) had a certified interpreter with her all the time then her proficiency level would be that of her hearing peers or even better. The coaches believed that they didn't have to coach my daughter. All she needed to do was watch and copy what she saw. Wrong! She needed to be coached and trained. She needed to understand why she did what she did and how to improve her technique. For example, without an interpreter how would Aaliyah know that she needed to tighten her butt muscles in order to offer more balance while doing a handstand? Okay maybe that's a funny example but I wanted my point to be something that can't be visualized (unless you wear extremely tight spandex). It has to be taught. Close your eyes for one moment and picture yourself being surrounded by people who speak a different language. How frustrated would you feel getting around in a strange city or even watching T.V.?

On a funnier note, earlier this year Aaliyah took a swim class in which there were 4 kids in the class and 3 spoke Spanish only. I was there, of course, for Aaliyah, but the 3 Spanish speaking children had no one. The instructor was all but 17 years old and usually had the deer in the headlights look when trying to teach a class of students who did not know what the heck he was talking about. At one point, the 3 kids started looking at me as if my signing would help them understand the class somehow. It really doesn't take a genius to see that deafness is not a disability but rather a culture with its own language and I am excited that my daughter is a part of it.

Although most of our problems with requests for interpreters come from recreational facilities, we have encountered problems with some medical facilities. A few years ago, at Aaliyah's pediatrician's office, I had requested an interpreter and was told that they usually had family members interpret. I informed the office manager that legally they were required to provide an interpreter under the ADA. The office manager said she would need to consult with their attorney regarding this matter and a few days later she called to inform me that I was right about my request. I told her that I was pleased to see that this was not going to be an issue and I could concentrate on being the concerned mom and not the interpreter at the office visits. After expressing my relief to the office manager, she replied, "Oh, the interpreter is not for you?" I wanted to put my hand through the phone and grab her by the collar and scream "Listen you idiot if I was deaf, would I be talking with you on the phone without the use of a relay service?" Eventually, after a few more conversations I was told that if I made appointments well in advance the office would be able to get an interpreter but for those appointments made on short notice this may not be possible. That was a start and thank goodness Aaliyah does not get sick a lot so short notice appointments would be rare.

Recently, Aaliyah had to go to physical therapy for problems she was having with her knees. I had set up 8 appointments 3 weeks before we were going to start therapy and requested an interpreter. I was told that this would be set up and then received a confirmation from the office that an interpreter was on the books for Aaliyah's appointments. Great! This request went well or so I thought. We ended up with no interpreter for the first 3 sessions but a lot of excuses. "Oh, we called but the agency said that they don't get paid for mileage." I am not sure why this was our concern but that was the excuse. "I'm not sure why the interpreter is not here, but I am going to complain to their supervisor." Yet another excuse and in the meantime I acted as Aaliyah's interpreter. This was fine but that wasn't the point. I wanted to be Aaliyah's mom and soak up all the information that was being passed out, not her interpreter.

On a positive note since the book's first release I wanted to add that we did go on a Disney World/ Disney Cruise vacation in the summer of 2005 and it was awesome. We spent 4 days on Disney World and all of the shows and most of the parades we saw were interpreted. Our days were structured around the interpreted events and required a great deal of planning. The reason for this is that Disney parks have designated days in which shows and parades are interpreted. Spontaneity was not an option for us and that would be the only thing that I would encourage Disney to change. Perhaps they could hire more interpreters so that a family could go to any park any day to watch any show. An interesting note was that at one of the interpreted parades we met one of the interpreters that ended up being our interpreter for the cruise. Aaliyah had 2 interpreters on the cruise. On the first day of the cruise we went over the activities that were offered and listed the ones that Aaliyah wanted to participate in and the interpreters were available for all them including the offshore excursions on Disney's Island.

On the last day of the cruise we had met an older couple who were both deaf, and they had not asked for an interpreter, however they were very excited to hear that the interpreters were on board and they ended up coming to the interpreted show even though they were assigned to see the later shows. The shows were wonderful and I found myself watching the interpreters in amazement. Their hands flowed with such grace and without hesitation. Overall, we loved the experience.

Perhaps if there were more incentives for businesses to make accommodations and if businesses were more educated about the needs of the deaf and hearing-impaired then requesting an interpreter would not be such a battle. At one point I had requested the assistance of a Deaf actor who lived in the area and his response to me was "Now you know what I go through." It was so nice to get such reassurance and help from him. It's too bad that this individual didn't think of how he could help future generations of deaf individuals avoid going through what he went through. Instead his approach was if I have to go through this so do you-Hah! I would definitely recommend that every parent with a Deaf child study the ADA in particular the ADA Guide for Small Businesses and areas of the ADA, which address auxiliary aids and effective communication with specific reference to sign language interpreters. The U.S. Department of Justice has ADA specialists available Monday through Friday that provide information about the ADA, answers to specific technical questions, free ADA materials, or information about filing a complaint by calling 1-800-514-0301(V) and 1-800-514-0383 (TTY). Remember to be an effective advocate for your child you need to know the laws that protect his or her rights.

Chapter 10

NEWS FLASH: Aaliyah Hears with Cochlear Implant

Preschool was coming to an end and Aaliyah was starting Kindergarten in the fall of 2000. She had worn her hearing aids consistently for two years without much benefit so it was time to consider a cochlear implant (CI). I knew about the Cochlear Implant Program at Children's Hospital in Seattle so I contacted the Program Coordinator and requested some information about their program and cochlear implants in general. I received the candidacy requirements for the cochlear implant, copies of articles with general information, and handouts about pediatric cochlear implants for parents. I also received a questionnaire and was asked to send back a copy of Aaliyah's most recent audiogram and IEP.

When I expressed my interest about cochlear implants to Aaliyah's teacher, she informed me that she was going through the candidacy process for a CI at another local hospital. Wow! I was a little shocked because from what I was told, the Deaf community didn't look upon cochlear implants positively. One belief is that receiving a cochlear implant should be the choice of the Deaf individual and parents should not be making that choice for their children. This only communicates the message that unless they are hearing they are inferior as a person. Some within the community believed that cochlear implants were a threat to extinction of the Deaf culture. They believed that hearing parents were unable to accept their deaf children and opted for the cochlear implant without exploring the possibilities of immersing their child in the deaf culture. Others felt that cochlear implants violated the integrity of the children's bodies and their human rights. They felt that CI's were barbaric, just like circumcision in girls.

It was very refreshing to meet a deaf individual who was willing to step away from the cultural beliefs related to cochlear implants and just do what felt right to her. Why would anyone object to a procedure that would make his or her life easier? I am all for not struggling and living as comfortably as I can so that is why I opted to have surgery to correct a visual impairment I had ever since the fifth grade. As I got older my vision seemed to get worse and at one point my husband pointed out that I had worn "coke bottle" glasses. In 1996, I had consulted with an eye doctor about LASIK eye surgery and after reviewing the literature they had sent me I felt that this was something I really wanted to do. It was becoming such a nuisance to wear glasses and to have Aaliyah grab at them all the time. Don't get me wrong, the thought of having surgery done on my eyes was really scary but the curiosity of what it would be like to live my life without glasses was an even stronger feeling.

I scheduled the appointment after a friend of mine offered to come with us since it would be a three-hour drive and my husband was away participating in military training. When we finally arrived to the clinic after a long drive of ambivalence, I felt somewhat reassured by the appearance of this huge 15 story building. As silly as it sounds coming from a nurse, I equated the doctor's success to this building because he must have been successful at what he did to own the whole building. Also, I am sure that the amount he charged for this procedure had an impact on his success. At the time, insurance companies were not covering the procedure and it had cost $1,500 for each eye. On the morning I had this done there were six other people waiting to go through this procedure and at $3,000 per person this doctor made $18,000 within one hour. Now that was amazing and it made me consider switching to a different profession. Well, that whole experience was entertaining now that I look back at it.

The procedure itself took five minutes and I wore a patch on both eyes for 24 hours. During that time I had a small taste and an appreciation for what the blind go through. It was challenging to care for Aaliyah and myself without sight. A few hours after the procedure, we went to a restaurant to grab a bite to eat and, as we entered the restaurant, I used my friend's shoulder as a guide to our table. After we finished our meal, my friend got up and took Aaliyah with her to pay for the meal but she forgot to hang around for me. I scurried behind her as best as I could without bumping into anyone or anything. As soon as she realized she had forgotten about me, my friend quickly came back to get me but I am sure we got some looks from the patrons. Again my surgery was not as involved as getting a cochlear implant but the results made my life easier and more enjoyable. Also, my curiosity related to seeing the world again without glasses really was a motivating factor in doing this. People want to live their lives with the least amount of obstacles as possible. It's only human nature to want life to be joyful and carefree even though obstacles tend to make us stronger individuals on how we approach life.

When Aaliyah's preschool teacher was asked why she wanted to hear and if she was really happy being deaf, her response was "When I get the CI and IF it is successful, then I will have the very best of BOTH worlds. This is what I want and this thought makes me even happier." There were many sounds the teacher wanted to hear with the cochlear implant. These included the car horn beeping, people's voices, her children calling her, the telephone ringing, fire drills, those deep conversations that her children have in the back seat of the car, birds, frogs, the waves of the ocean, and the wind in the trees. She said that if she was able to hear just some of these sounds then it would have been worth getting a cochlear implant. She was asked many questions from those around her who were curious and not afraid to bombard her with the following questions:

Q: Will you still sign?
A: Of course!
Q: Will your children still sign?
A: I spent ten years teaching them....so, YES!
Q: Can I have your Deaf equipment?
A: NO, (chuckle) because I will still need it at night time when the speech processor is not on me.
Q: What have they predicted that you will be able to hear?
A: Environmental sounds, peoples' voices, many sounds like wind in the tree's, birds, walking on leaves and rocks, some music, the refrigerator, dogs barking, airplanes, people calling my name- if its not too noisy.
Q: What about the DEAF COMMUNITY?
A: So far everyone that I have told has been, well, surprised and also curious. My friends are waiting to see what I can or can not hear with it.
Q: What will you call yourself? Deaf or Hard of Hearing?

A: I will call myself "Deaf with a CI". This is because being Deaf is much more than just having a profound hearing loss. It's the use of ASL and your feelings about being Deaf.

Q: Do you hate being Deaf then?

A: OF COURSE NOT! I am happy as a Deaf person but my constant curiosity about what it is like to hear is killing me! Smile!

Not only was this moment important for the teacher but also for me because I learned from her experience and it prepared Aaliyah and myself for what was to come. There were many questions I had related to the implant and I made sure that they were all answered. The one thing I did know for sure was that even though Children's Hospital was not the only hospital with a Cochlear Implant Program, I knew from my past nursing experience that this was the best place for a child to have surgery because there were pediatric specialists available.

On May 15, 2000 I finally had my consultation with the Program Coordinator and was given an extensive amount of material including: cochlear implant options, evaluation procedures, the CI's impact on Aaliyah's hearing, speech, and language, surgery and post-implant procedures, and cost of the implant. Many if not all of the following questions were answered. How does a CI work? What are the different types of implants available? How much does a CI cost? Will my insurance cover this? What are the risks involved? What happens during surgery? How long is surgery? How long is the recovery period? What is the follow-up like? How successful is the CI? What will Aaliyah hear? What have been the experiences of other children who have received a CI?

I received a contact list of families with children who received cochlear implants. I was informed that Aaliyah would need to be evaluated by other professionals on the cochlear implant team to include the surgeon, the aural rehabilitation specialist, and a psychologist. Finally, if we decided to go through with the surgery there would be a team meeting to discuss the results of all the tests and evaluations and make recommendations.

After the consultation, I studied all the information I had received from the program coordinator and other resources. Perhaps after reading this chapter some might say that I didn't do enough research and yet perhaps there are those that would say I researched too much. I felt that in my heart I researched enough material to make the best choice for Aaliyah. Now, it had been many, many, years since my anatomy and physiology class in nursing school so I forgot the exact details on the workings of the inner ear even though I understood how the CI worked.

How does our ear work? First sound is transmitted as sound waves in the air and enters the outer ear. After entering the outer ear, sound waves move along the ear canal until they hit the end of the canal, which is covered by the eardrum. The eardrum vibrates causing the three tiny bones on the other side of the eardrum to vibrate also. These bones are the smallest bones in the body. As these three tiny bones vibrate, this causes the fluid in the inner ear or cochlea to move. The cochlea is the part of the ear that lets you hear sounds. One end of the cochlea detects low frequencies and the other end detects high frequencies. It looks like a snail shell and is comprised of three canals, which are lined with many little hairs. The hairs stand up in rows and each one is connected to the hearing nerve. The movement of the inner ear fluid causes the hair cells in the cochlea to bend. When touched, the hair cells send a signal to the hearing nerve, which in turn tells your brain that you hear something.

The hair cells within Aaliyah's cochlea were either missing or damaged and therefore they could not send sound wave messages to the hearing nerve. Unlike hearing aids, a CI would not make sounds louder for her but would directly stimulate the surviving hearing nerve fibers in her cochlea, allowing her to perceive sounds.

A CI consists of two parts: an internal component and an external component. The internal component is the part of the system that is surgically implanted under the skin behind the ear, and is referred to as the implant. The external components include the speech processor, a cable and a headpiece.

The internal component consists of electronic circuits and a long thin, flexible tube called an electrode array. The electronic circuit is then placed surgically in a shallow crevice made in the bone behind the ear. The electrode array is then threaded into the cochlea and is used to deliver stimulation to the hearing nerve. When the electrodes are activated, a CI can stimulate different parts of the cochlea and thus conveys different frequencies of sound called channels.

The external component is the part that is worn outside the body in a pocket harness, on a belt or behind the ear like a hearing aid and is called the speech processor. The speech processor contains a microphone and a computer, which is used to send the electrical sound information to the implant.

Although all CI systems are composed of the internal and external components, the technology is different between the three manufacturers. There have been three major manufacturers which market systems that have been approved by the FDA for general sales in the United States. Advanced Bionics the makers of the Clarion has their headquarters and manufacturing facilities located in the United States. Cochlear Corporation, the makers of the Nucleus, houses its headquarters and manufacturing facilities in Australia. Lastly, Med-El has its headquarters and manufacturing facilities in Austria.

In the summer of 2000, Children's Hospital had three types of CI systems available from two of the three manufacturers: The Nucleus 22 and Nucleus 24 Cochlear Implant Systems and the Clarion Cochlear Implant Systems. Children's Hospital participated in the clinical trials for both the Nucleus 24 and the Clarion implants, and felt strongly that both devices provided significant benefit to children. The Clarion Cochlear Implant was approved for use in children in July of 1997 and the Nucleus 24 Channel Cochlear Implant system was approved for use in children in 1998. Children's was also actively participating in a clinical trial with the Nucleus 24 Contour Cochlear Implant System. The Nucleus 24 Contour Implant system was investigational which meant that the FDA allowed its use only in research. The internal part was being investigated while the external part was already FDA approved and on the market.

The Cochlear Implant Program Coordinator was very objective in the information she presented on both systems. She offered hands on models of the different systems and this gave me a chance to actually see the systems up close instead of pictures in a book which was extremely helpful in the decision making process. I understood that each system had their strengths and weaknesses but I based my decision on the three features mentioned below.

The first difference between the two systems was their appearance. I liked the sleek look and curved edges of the Nucleus' speech processor to the boxy look of the Clarion. I also felt that the internal component of the Nucleus's system, which is the part that actually goes under the skin, looked smaller and thinner. From what I was told and the information I read, the Nucleus simplified surgery because less drilling was required to create the crevice in which the internal component would lie.

The second difference between the two systems was the number of electrodes that each system had. Remember the electrodes are what provides electrical stimulation to the hearing nerve endings and create sound sensations. As the CI stimulates an electrode on a certain part of the cochlea this in turn conveys different frequency of sounds. The Nucleus 24 Contour had 22 electrodes and 22 channels. This meant that there were potentially 22 different sites of the cochlea that could be stimulated. The Clarion had 16 electrode contacts and eight channels. In theory, the more electrodes a system has the more channels (a distinct sound frequency) it should be able to deliver. The more channels the better because this gives you more options for choosing more responsive hearing nerve fibers, providing more pitch information, and improving hearing in noise. Also, especially in children, if the implant can provide at least eight or more channels of stimulation, then word recognition and language acquisition would be significantly facilitated.

The third difference and perhaps the key to my final decision was that I was told that the Nucleus 24 Contour system caused less damage to residual hearing than the other systems. This was accomplished because the Nucleus 24 Contour system had a self-curling electrode that caused less damage when inserted into the cochlea and this in turn provided a better fit. Granted Aaliyah did not have much residual hearing to begin with but the nurse in me thought that it was better to go with a system that caused the least amount of damage and had the potential to have the greatest benefit.

What would Aaliyah hear with the cochlear implant? If the surgery and device setting was successful then she might be able to respond to tones at approximately 30-40 dB on an audiogram. This meant that conversation as well as other moderately soft sounds in the environment would be heard. Wow! Remember Aaliyah's hearing had consistently been between 65 - 100dB. What a difference! I realized that the surgery did not guarantee hearing for her within the 30-40 dB range, but I thought whatever hearing she was able to receive was an improvement. Although her hearing would not be considered normal to the hearing person, the sounds she would hear after the implant would eventually be considered normal to her after she clearly learned to make associations with those sounds. Also, just because she would hear sounds didn't mean that she would understand speech by listening alone. With practice, she might be able to recognize some environmental sounds, words from a small set of pictures, and/or words by listening. Her lip-reading ability may also improve with the use of the cochlear implant.

How would the implant affect Aaliyah's speech? Results vary from child to child. I learned that children with cochlear implants might develop more control over their speech which meant that Aaliyah might be able to turn her voice on and off more easily; she might have better control over the loudness of her voice, and her voice may be less nasal sounding and less high pitched.

After receiving a very thorough explanation as to the benefits Aaliyah might receive from the cochlear implant, I couldn't really find a reason not to go ahead with the surgery. However, I was a little hesitant about the surgery itself because Aaliyah never had any kind of surgery up to this point and I knew there would be risks involved. Even though being a nurse helped me through this period, it was a burden in one sense because of my experience.

What happens during surgery for an implant? The surgery would take three hours and the child is given general anesthesia. An IV is started for fluids and any medications that need to be given. A tube is then placed in the child's throat to help with breathing during the surgical procedure. The area behind the ear that will be operated on is cleansed and the hair is shaved. The surgeon will make an incision behind the ear in the skin basically causing a flap that can be lifted back. This allows the surgeon to see the bone in which a well will be created by drilling. This well will hold the receiver-stimulator. Once this has been done, the surgeon's attention is then placed on the cochlea. A hole is drilled into cochlea so that the electrode array can be threaded through it. Finally, the skin flap is brought back down and stitched. Antibiotic ointment is placed on the site and a pressure bandage is applied. The child's anesthesia is reversed and the tube that had been placed in the throat is removed. The child is then transferred to the recovery room. The amount of time needed to stay in the hospital after surgery varies but the stay can be as short as 1-2 days or in rare instances ten or more days.

What happens after surgery? Immediately following surgery, parents need to be prepared for what their child may look like. The child will have a large bandage on his head, an IV in his arm, a partially shaved head (at the incision site, which may be covered by the bandage), an incision, and maybe some swelling. The child may experience dizziness and/or nausea and vomiting from the anesthesia. After the anesthesia has worn off then some pain may set in. Four to six weeks after surgery, the cochlear implant is turned on and at that time the child receives stimulation through the implant. I was told that some children are startled by the sound and may experience feelings ranging from joy to inquisitiveness to fear while others may not respond at all in the beginning.

After the device is turned on, each electrode must be programmed or "mapped". During a mapping session, the child's speech processor is connected directly to a computer, which uses a special program and allows the audiologist to determine the "threshold -or softest sound" (T-level) and the "comfort level-or the most comfortable loud sound" (C-Level) for each electrode implanted in the child's inner ear. This information is then stored in the speech processor and is called a MAP, which gets fine-tuned at each visit until a stable MAP is established.

In order to obtain the most stable MAP for a particular child, mapping is done frequently in the beginning. A schedule may be that the child comes to the clinic for 1-2 hours, 2 or 3 times in the first week, then 1-2 times in the second week, then once a month for the first 6 months. Mapping will then decrease in frequency to every 6 months for the next 2 years after which the electrodes will be checked annually.

Along with mapping, the child's performance with the device is monitored on a regular basis. An audiological assessment will be done every 3 months for the first year, every 6 months for the next 2 years and annually after that. Communication and developmental assessments of the child will occur every 6 months for the first year and annually thereafter. In addition, a psychological assessment is done 3-6 months and 18 months after the device is turned on.

What have been the experiences of some children that have received a CI? At a sign language conference I attended, I heard that a teenager had gotten an implant and chose not to wear it. Apparently, the teenager had the usual body image issues that all adolescents go through and wanted to fit in with her deaf friends. In another situation a young child had received a CI and the parents didn't follow through with the follow up appointments so the child was not able to reap the benefits of the CI. Overall, I was told that most of the younger children in the program adapted well to the implant because it just became a part of them and their daily routine like wearing hearing aids.

Finally decision time came as I sat down with my husband to review all the information. My husband said that if I felt that this was something I truly believed could work for Aaliyah than he would go along with it. I knew this was the right thing to do at the time but even though my husband was willing to go along with the decision, he had reservations about the surgery. He would make comforting comments like "I hope nothing happens to my baby." Having such responsibility put on me, made this period extremely stressful. I worried day and night from the moment I gave the go ahead for the surgery until months after the surgery. What if something did happened to her, not only would I blame myself but my husband would also blame me. I don't think I would have handled that situation very well. Matter of fact, I am sure I would have had a nervous breakdown.

I notified the Cochlear Implant Coordinator that I wanted Aaliyah to get the Nucleus 24 Contour System. She promptly set up a pre-cochlear implant visit as well as a team meeting on June 30, 2000. At the training visit Aaliyah was shown a "demo" cochlear implant and was allowed to handle the equipment. She was somewhat familiar with the equipment because her teacher at school had recently received an implant. After this appointment, Aaliyah and I took a tour of the hospital and then the team meeting took place.

At the team meeting results of a sedated CT scan and MRI, an auditory skills assessment, and a psychological consultation on expectations of the CI were reviewed and based on this review Aaliyah's candidacy for a cochlear implant was decided. Besides us, the team members present at the meeting included the Cochlear Implant Coordinator; the Pediatric Otolaryngologist-who would be performing the surgery, the Aural Rehabilitation Specialist, and the Psychologist. Was Aaliyah a good candidate for the cochlear implant? At the time her candidacy was being evaluated, a general profile of a candidate consisted of the following:

1. The child is 18 months and older.
2. The child's has a severe-to-profound hearing loss in both ears.
3. The child has a normal cochlea by a CT scan.
4. The child has a reliable audiogram.
5. The child demonstrates little or no benefit from consistent hearing aid use.

Other considerations for a successful candidate included:

1. A supportive family with realistic expectations.
2. Children who lost hearing after they were born.
3. Duration of deafness being less than 2 years.
4. No multiple handicaps.
5. No evidence of severe organic brain damage.
6. No evidence of mental retardation.
7. No behavioral-personality traits that would make completion of the rehabilitation program unlikely.

Today, children as young as 12 months old are being implanted. Believe it or not, I have even come across some literature about the possibility of implanting babies with the world's first totally implantable cochlear implant.

Ultimately, the success of a child with a cochlear implant depends on family involvement, which is another important criterion considered when looking at candidacy for implantation. A family must be able to support the child and follow through with recommendations throughout the assessment and rehabilitation process. Parents must have realistic expectations and understand that the cochlear implant does not restore normal hearing. Also, parents must be aware that what their child will hear and how well their speech will be is highly variable and unpredictable. This criterion was in place when Aaliyah was considered and remains unchanged to date.

After reviewing the evaluations, the team members agreed that Aaliyah was an excellent candidate for a cochlear implant. It was decided that her right ear would be implanted since the left ear was considered her better ear. Usually the better ear is not implanted because it is thought that if for whatever reason the implant does not work than the better ear is still left intact. The following report was written. "Aaliyah has no medical or audiological contraindications regarding cochlear implantation. Factors that indicate Aaliyah would do well with a CI include her young age, normal cochlea and internal auditory canal by CT scan, and absence of multiple handicaps. In addition, the fact that Aaliyah has consistent hearing aid use, established weekly auditory and speech therapy, good language development, and excellent family involvement makes her a good candidate for a cochlear implant."

Once Aaliyah was approved as a candidate, no time was wasted in scheduling her surgery and placing the pre-authorization to the insurance company. Aaliyah's surgery was scheduled for July 7, 2000. Great! We made it this far without any problems. Nothing could go wrong, right?

I will be perfectly honest and say that the thought of not being able to afford a cochlear implant for Aaliyah never crossed my mind because she was covered under my husband's health insurance plan with Premera Blue Cross as well as my plan with Regence Blue Shield. Through my experiences at work with health insurance companies, these two companies were considered two of the better ones. As we always had done in the past with medical services provided, I thought we would pay our deductible and the two companies would pay for the rest. Imagine my surprise when I received a letter from Regence Blue Shield on June 20th. "Your preauthorization request has been reviewed and it has been determined that the cochlear implant cannot be approved. The reason for this is because cochlear implants are specifically excluded by the member's health plan". I immediately called the Cochlear Implant Coordinator to discuss this and was reassured that everything would be just fine. The program would send over all the documentation necessary to show medical necessity for the CI. I was also reminded that we still would be receiving a reply from my husband's health insurance plan. After our conversation, I felt a little better but I was still nervous. I hated playing this waiting game. Would this game continue up to the day before surgery? Were we getting ready to get on an insurance roller coaster only to find out we would not be able to get the CI. I have to say it really sucks not to be filthy rich when it comes to situations like this. I am sure Bill Gates doesn't have to worry whether or not his family can afford medical care.

A few days later I got more bad news. My husband's health insurance carrier also denied approval for the CI for the same reason. The cochlear implant was specifically excluded by his plan and so the drama continued. Again, I called the CI Coordinator nearly in tears but she continued to reassure me that everything would work out in the end. She stated that my health insurance carrier still needed to review the documentation that was sent to them and that she would send the same documentation to my husband's health insurance carrier so that they may review all the documentation necessary for the CI.

In the meantime, the Coordinator suggested that I talk with the hospital's Patient Financial Specialist who would be able to help us look at other possible options to pay for the surgery. The cost of Aaliyah receiving a Cochlear Implant would be around $40,000. We made an appointment with the Financial Specialist on June 29th during the time Aaliyah would be recovering from a sedated MRI. Apparently, the head CT that she had done was not as clear as the surgeon would have liked. This would be the last thing Aaliyah would need to get done before the surgery itself and it went well.

During the MRI, Aaliyah was asleep but I think I left with a mild hearing loss because even though I wore earplugs I could still hear the loud galloping sound afterwards. As I sat in the room where Aaliyah was recovering from the sedation, I met with the Financial Specialist. She explained the two options we could look into to assist us in paying for the surgery not including what our insurance plan may cover. One option was to apply for financial medical assistance from the state. However, after I gave her information about our family income she felt that we probably would not qualify.

The second option we had was to apply for financial assistance through Children's Hospital Uncompensated Care Fund. The Financial Specialist was very confident that we would qualify for this. She explained that the money in this fund is collected from the donations received through the annual telethon Children's Hospital sponsors on TV. I always wondered were that money went. She told me that what the insurance would not cover the hospital would pay for the rest. If the insurance company would not cover any of the cost, Children's Hospital would cover the whole amount and we would not have to pay anything out of our pocket.

Also, by receiving this assistance from the hospital, Aaliyah would receive free care through the hospital until she was 18. This included any medical service including speech therapy. The only thing this did not cover was dental services unless it was an emergency. The only requirement to receive this ongoing care was to apply annually for this assistance. I was really shocked to hear this since I had become accustomed to hear that our income disqualified us for many state services. I certainly never expected Children's to cover the cost of a $40,000 procedure. Well, lets just say I was truly flabbergasted and relieved. Aaliyah woke up from the sedation and as soon as she was stable enough to leave the hospital, we headed back home. This was a great day.

On June 30th, we finally did receive a letter from my health insurance plan stating, "The medical necessity for the cochlear implant has been established but the cochlear implant will not be added as a covered benefit on this member's plan until the group renews on December 1, 2000." Not that this mattered but it was nice to know that the insurance was going to cover this in DECEMBER. Well, a few days later I received a letter from Children's Hospital stating that we were approved to receive financial assistance from them and that we would be responsible for 0% of the charges. Things were definitely on the up swing. To everyone's amazement, the day before Aaliyah's surgery, my husband's insurance company sent an approval over the fax. They approved coverage for the Cochlear Implant and Children's would be covering the rest. Now that the insurance stuff was out of the way we could begin focusing on preparing for surgery day, July 7, 2000.

Months before the surgery, Aaliyah's Grandmother and Uncle informed us they would be visiting us the first two weeks of July. This was before we had told them that Aaliyah would be having surgery on July 7th. What a coincidence that they planned their visit the same time Aaliyah was scheduled to have her surgery. God wanted family to be with us during this time and it was wonderful. I was excited and happy about their visit.

A few days after our family arrived, we started calling around to see if there were any motor homes for rent. Although, I knew that I would stay with Aaliyah at the hospital, we wanted to have all of our family near her during and after the surgery. A motor home would be the perfect solution and the hospital had an area of the parking lot designated for motor homes. After calling around to numerous places, we were unable to locate a motor home to rent but two days prior to Aaliyay's surgery, my husband called me from work to let me know that his boss was going to let us borrow his motor home. This was great because now all of us could go up to the hospital. The day before the surgery, we packed up the motor home and later that evening I gave Aaliyah a bath and made sure she ate and drank a little something before she settled for the night since she could not have anything to eat or drink after midnight. All five of us (Aaliyah, her dad, grandmother, uncle, and myself) got comfortable for the night in the motor home and left the house to begin our journey to Seattle's Children's Hospital.

We arrived at the hospital around 10 p.m. and registered our car. We hooked up the motor home to a designated site in the parking lot. There were only two other motor homes in the parking lot besides ours. I have to say if you are going to spend a couple of days at the hospital for whatever the reason, the motor home is a much more comfortable way to go rather than spending every minute in the hospital. You are close enough to run back and forth if anything does happen. We were pretty tired and had no problem going to sleep. It was nice to know that the next morning all we had to do was wake up in the morning and walk across the parking lot to get things started.

Surgery day arrived early in the morning on July 7th. We walked across the parking lot to the hospital to register Aaliyah for her surgery. A sign language interpreter was waiting for us when we arrived. While we waited, we colored pictures, read some books, and played with some of the games that were in the waiting room. Two hours had gone by and I was getting somewhat annoyed because Aaliyah still had not had anything to eat or drink since Midnight. I went up to the nurse's station to ask what was taking so long and she explained that there was an emergency. Finally, it was Aaliyah's turn to go back into the preoperative area that prepares you for the surgery but the interpreter had to leave because she was told she would only be needed for the two hours. Well, I ended up playing interpreter, which was fine. Aaliyah got dressed in the hospital gown and got her weight, temperature and blood pressure taken. The nurse asked me some questions related to Aaliyah's medical history and if she ever had blood work done to see if she had the disease or trait for sickle cell anemia. When I said no, she said that this would be necessary since Aaliyah was biracial (African-American and White).

The nurse also asked me if I would like Aaliyah's DNA examined to see if there were any genetic reasons for her deafness since there were several hundred genes known to cause hereditary hearing loss and deafness. The nurse thought that this information might be useful to us if we plan to have more children. Well, we were not planning to have any more children so I declined.

What good would this information do me? It would not change the fact that Aaliyah was deaf. I thought this test should be Aaliyah's choice when the time was right for her.

After getting her blood drawn, the pediatric anesthesiologist came into the room and asked questions about Aaliyah's medical history. Again, I thought. I guess this was pay back for all those times I was that second or third person to ask a parent to repeat their concerns for the doctor. The anesthesiologist told me that Aaliyah would be receiving general anesthesia in the form of a gas through a mask that would put her to sleep. After all questions were asked and answered, the nurse told us it was time to bring Aaliyah to an area where she would be giving her "sleeping gas." As she laid on the gurney, she picked which scented gas she wanted. She signed that she wanted the bubble gum flavor and the mask was placed over her mouth and nose. The doctor had her count to 10 and at three she had a huge smile on her face. Her arms were floating in the air as she waved her hand in front of us and signed, "I love you." My husband and I told her how much we loved her and gave her a big kiss. She never did reach 10. Sound asleep; she was wheeled away from us. We headed back to the nurse's station where we were given a pager and told that the surgery would take about three hours and we would be paged when Aaliyah was out of surgery. Since there was no interpreter available I was told that I would be allowed to meet her in the recovery room so I could be there when she woke up even though parents were not allowed to see their kids until they were awake in the recovery room or on the floor. We went to grab a bite to eat in the hospital cafeteria and then went back to the motor home to sit and wait.

Back in the motor home things were tense and quiet. We all prayed that everything would go well. Silence certainly can breed negative thinking in a situation such as this but the nurse in me knew that Aaliyah was in the best place for this surgery even though the mother in me was still worried. If anything happened to her I would never forgive myself for putting her in the situation. I think I went through 20 cups of coffee waiting to be paged. I walked back and forth to the hospital stretching my legs. The three-hour mark was near but the pager had not gone off. All of us were getting concerned so my husband and I went back to the nurse's station and asked how much longer it would be before we could see her. The nurse told us that they had been buzzing us for a while but apparently the pager was not working. I guess it would make too much sense to check these pagers before giving them to the parents).

We were furious but remained calm because we just wanted to know where our baby was. The nurses told us that she had been brought to the recovery room and so off we rushed to find her. Excited emotions filled our hearts only to be extinguished by the recovery room nurse who told us "Oh, Aaliyah was brought to the general surgery floor, she's still asleep and doing fine." Feeling like lab rates in an experimental maze scouring to get that piece of cheese, we once again took off trying to get to Aaliyah's room before she woke up. When we got to the floor, the nurse walked us to Aaliyah's room and she was still asleep. What a relief! I really wanted to be there when she woke up. Even though she laid there with this huge bandage wrapped around her ear and head, dry lips and swollen face, she looked comfortable. She also had an IV hooked up to her hand for fluids since she would not be drinking for awhile. We were by her side for a while, when her grandmother and uncle arrived. An hour or so later, the surgeon came up to the floor and explained that the surgery went well. They had to shave a small amount of her hair behind her right ear. The surgeon said that Aaliyah lost a minimal amount of blood and her facial nerve was monitored throughout the procedure and appeared to be undamaged. Also, the implant was tested to make sure that it worked. The plan was to discharge her the next day if she was getting up to go to the bathroom, walking around, and drinking enough fluids so that the IV could be removed.

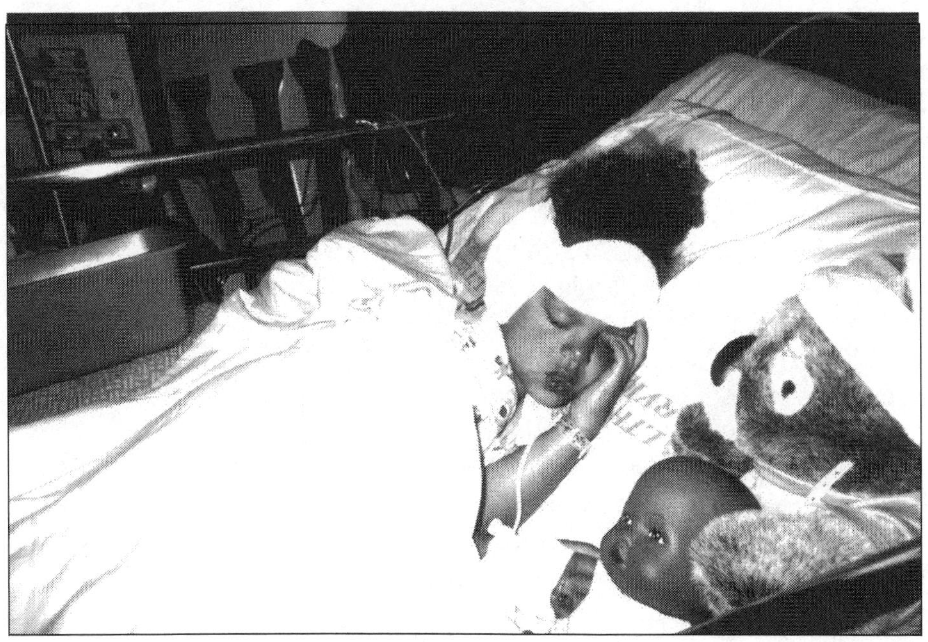

Aaliyah the day of the Cochlear Implant surgery in July 2000.

A feeling of relief embraced me and I thanked God that everything went well during surgery. Aaliyah spent most of the day asleep, only opening her eyes periodically. At one point, she was awake long enough to eat some ice chips. She remained fairly comfortable during the day only requiring pain medication twice. She vomited twice that day and started getting up more that evening to go to the bathroom. Since she slept all day, that night she ate a popsicle and we were up a few times walking the halls. When she finally went to sleep, I slept beside her in one of those super uncomfortable hospital chairs that pull out to a bed. This didn't last very long because she woke up a couple of times and tried to crawl over the bed railings to sleep next to me. In order to prevent her from injuring herself, the nurse said that it was O.K. for me to sleep in the hospital bed with Aaliyah. What a relief for my back!

The next day Aaliyah continued to recover well and she kept her breakfast down and was up and moving around. The plan was for her to be discharged after the surgeon saw her progress later that morning and wrote discharge orders. The nurse came in and began to talk to us about the medications Aaliyah would need to take as well as what we were to watch for as far as complications. She would need to take a liquid antibiotic twice a day for 10 days, pain medication every 4-6 hours if she needed it, and an antibiotic ointment applied to her incision three times a day for 10 days. We were instructed to call her doctor if any of the following symptoms developed: high fever, any redness, swelling or drainage from the incision, if the pain medication was not helping, if nausea or vomiting was not helped by dietary changes and if any dizziness occurred that interfered with her daily routine. We were told to keep her ear dry for one week and then we could wash her hair. Most importantly, we had to protect the surgical site from trauma so Aaliyah would have to wear a protective covering with a bandage over the site around the clock for 2-3 days and then only at night for one week.

The surgeon had arrived and saw how well Aaliyah was doing so she told us that we could go home if we wanted. We took her up on that offer and got ready to go home. Aaliyah's bandage was changed and she was given a hard plastic protective covering the shape of a bowl with a gauze bandage inside for her surgical site. This protective covering stayed in place with a strap that was wrapped around her head and fastened with Velcro. I helped her get dressed and her IV was removed. Since we had a drive ahead of us she was given pain medicine to keep her comfortable for the trip back home.

Aaliyah the day after surgery.

The first two weeks after the implant went well. I took off from work and Aaliyah was on summer vacation so she didn't miss any school and we were able to really concentrate on taking it easy. Aaliyah required pain medication perhaps one to two times a day for the first three days we were at home. She completed her 10-day course of liquid antibiotics as well as the antibiotic ointment that we diligently applied to her incision. Aaliyah was very protective about her surgical site and wore her protective gear daily. I would say she wore that thing for about one month, much longer then was instructed by the surgeon. I think this was her security blanket and from the minute she woke up she wanted to wear the protective gear until she got settled for the night. The only reason she stopped wearing it was because one day it just disappeared. I wonder where that thing went.

One month after the surgery Aaliyah was scheduled to get her implant turned on and the incision behind her right ear was healing nicely. The only thing we felt was a small bump where the implant was. Her hair was also starting to grow back and since her hair was long and curly you could not tell that some of her hair was shaven. She was not having any trouble with facial nerve paralysis or with things tasting funny. Aaliyah's teacher told me that after her implant, foods tasted very metallic on one side of her tongue.

The day finally came to have her implant turned on. At this appointment we would receive the speech processor, all the accessories that went along with it, and finally got to see what she could hear. Was this surgery successful? Yes, she was healing nicely from the surgery itself but would she be able to hear something? I needed confirmation. I felt the same as I did at her first audiogram after she got her hearing aids. The audiologist only activated 11 of the 22 electrodes because she didn't want to make the experience uncomfortable for Aaliyah. As the electrodes were being activated the only noticeable response I could see on Aaliyah's face was that her eyes opened wider as she turned her head to me with a look that said, "Wow, I can hear that!" It didn't look like the experience was painful and she was able to tell the audiologist when the speech processor was turned on and off. At one point there were some musical instrument that were brought out for her to play with. She began banging the instruments, trying to make the loudest sounds she possibly could. She pounded her fists on the table and stomped her feet in order to make different sounds. It looked like she enjoyed hearing the sounds she was making.

Two days after this appointment, we went back for more mapping and to get the remaining electrodes activated. I told the audiologist that Aaliyah was somewhat resistant to wearing her implant for lengthy periods of time but was willing to wear it for one hour here and there and I praised her during those times.

One week after having her implant turned on Aaliyah had her first audiogram. All I can say is that it was truly amazing. Yes, two days earlier I saw that she could hear sounds but now I had proof on paper. The surgery worked! It really worked! She responded to sounds at 45 dB, which is a level that approximates soft conversational speech. These results indicated that she detected sounds in the mild to moderate hearing loss range with the cochlear implant. Mild to moderate hearing loss, can you believe it! On the audiogram her responses were now graphed in the middle of the chart not at the bottom lower left portion. Another audiogram would need to be repeated in one month.

Born to be wild at Ocean Shores, Aug 2000

Aaliyah enjoying Summer 2000

Aaliyah at a friend's Hawaiian B-day party, Aug 2000

The school year had arrived and Aaliyah started kindergarten, not only with new clothes and a big girl attitude but also with this new ability to hear. Right from day one we started a daily routine. When Aaliyah woke up in the morning, I would give her about one hour to get in wake up mode before I put her speech processor on. Her preschool teacher had told me that when she would turn her implant on in the morning at times it was uncomfortable just as if she had walked into a room with a bright light shining in her eyes. A few minutes before leaving the house I would put her speech processor on, turn on the implant and make sure that her equipment was functioning properly. Once we left the house she had about 30 minutes to adjust to her implant, which was already on before we got to school. She wore her implant at school all day every day without any resistance but at home she would take it off. I didn't push the issue at home because I didn't want her to hate the implant. I thought that eventually we would work up to wearing it at home all day on weekends and during vacations. It had only been about 1-½ months since Aaliyah's implant was turned on.

While at school, Aaliyah wore the body worn processor on a belt that was worn over her clothes. She didn't like the harness that was recommended for children and I wanted something sturdier than just wearing it around her waist so I sewed pockets on the back of hers tee shirts that she wore under her shirts. This allowed easy access to the processor and kept it securely in place. Since I didn't know how to sew on actual pockets, I took one of her socks and sewed it on the back of her tee shirt. The toe portion of the sock was on the bottom and the top was left open to slide the processor into. This provided a nice stable cushion around the processor so she could run, tumble, and climb without having the processor get in the way. Aaliyah actually wore these tee shirts for the first year and a half after getting the processor. As she got used to having the implant she wanted to be responsible for her processor and wanted it in front on a belt so she could watch the screen and make sure it was functioning properly.

For a kindergartner, Aaliyah's schedule was quite full. She went to school all day Monday through Friday and to Children's Hospital's Aural Rehabilitation Clinic every Monday for speech therapy. On Thursdays, she went to another speech therapist. Don't forget Aaliyah had mappings, follow-up appointment with the surgeon and audiograms also scheduled throughout the months. Was this too much for her? At times I felt that this was too much for the both of us. It wasn't fair that my baby had to do all these things while her hearing peers didn't. There were other times that I thought all of this would be well worth it when Aaliyah was a successful adult not struggling to adapt to her world and she would actually thank me for being an involved mom. Occasionally, I would receive negative comments from my mother about not letting Aaliyah be a kid because she was to busy with appointments. Well, I refused to let these comments get me down.

Aaliyah had her second audiogram done one month after the initial hook up and the results showed that she heard at 30 dB, which indicated that she detected sounds in the mild hearing loss range, better than the previous results. This also meant that average conversational speech was accessible to her. She learned to use her hearing more and more and the audiograms consistently reported results between 30 to 35 dB (mild hearing loss range). I have been asked many times "Can she hear now with the implant?" The best way I know how to answer this is that Aaliyah hears most of the sounds I hear in the sound booth during the audiograms. She may miss some of the softer sounds but generally she hears a lot of the sounds that I can hear. Since she has only had her implant implant for eight years now, her hearing ability is that of an 8-year-old hearing child. I have to remind people that sounds we are used to hearing don't sound the same to her. For example, when I hear a bird chirping it does not sound the same way to Aaliyah. However, after hearing that particular sound many times she will associate it to a bird chirping. She will constantly need to learn the meaning behind the sounds she hears.

Aaliyah's progress with the cochlear implant was very slow but exciting. She used her voice much more as she signed. Sometimes I wondered if she went to bed with sore hands and mouth because she was and continues to be such a chatterbox. Her lip reading skills improved and when we played games such as spelling bee bingo, I would say the letters without signing them. She knew which letter I said 98% of the time and when I read to her, I would sign "Where is the... and then say boy without signing it to see if Aaliyah understood what I said. Again she was usually 95% accurate. It was truly amazing to see her responses to the hearing games we played. One game we played involved Aaliyah's back being turned to me and I would call her name. When she heard her name, she raised her hand and got it every time. Interestingly, during normal interactions at home if I called her name there were more times that she didn't respond possibly because she was distracted by the TV or playing.

As the school year progressed, Aaliyah began to respond to her name more than 50% of the time. Her spontaneous vocalizations increased in frequency and improved in accuracy. She constantly used her voice when she communicated and her vocabulary exploded. Although she wore her body worn processor about 6-7 hours a day Monday through Friday, we continued to encourage her to wear her implant for certain activities such as going to the movies, listening to music, or playing computer games that required her to listen. Her attitude toward the implant remained indifferent as if she could take it or leave it.

Prior to starting the second grade, Aaliyah had the same teacher, classroom, and classmates for three years. I had been extremely happy with the consistency of the school program. I really believe that consistency and structure at home as well as school is essential for school age children. They need to have a routine in order to be successful in their educational endeavors. If their lives are filled with chaos, they don't do as well in school and usually end up with behavioral issues. It is our responsibility as parents to make sure that time is set aside everyday for homework, dinner as a family, family time, and a decent bedtime. Although these three years at school had little change in the routinc, Aaliyah started the second grade with some exciting new changes, which included a behind the ear speech processor (BTE), a bigger classroom and a few missing front teeth. She received her BTE just before school started which meant that she no longer had to wear the body worn processor. The BTE which looked similar to a hearing aid had a compartment that housed the hearing aid type batteries and had twelve different colors that Aaliyah could match with whatever outfit she was wearing for that day.

I was so excited when Aaliyah got the BTE because I hoped she would be more motivated to wear her cochlear implant everyday and not just for school. However, I was wrong and again I struggled daily with the issue of insisting that she wear the BTE more often than she did just as I had with her hearing aids. As with the hearing aids, I didn’t want her to hate the implant so I continued to praise her when she wore it and encouraged her to wear it at other times. For example, one evening when we went to a Broadway performance of Beauty and the Beast I explained to her that there would be a lot of music and singing and if she wanted to hear any of it she would need to wear her implant. She tried but thirty minutes into the performance she asked to take the implant off because the sounds were too loud for her. I was really hoping she would want to wear the implant for the whole performance because the music was so beautiful (to me) but perhaps to her it was just a bunch of loud sounds. Well, whatever the reason I praised her for wearing the CI for that brief time.

Second grade was not only a time for exciting changes for Aaliyah but it was a time of hard work for me because I had to really fight for her to have the same teacher and classmates. August was a very tense time for me and I felt as if I had an ongoing ulcer thanks to the money hungry, inflexible and insensitive school administrators I had to deal with. I informed Aaliyah's old school district, the Tacoma School District, that we had a change in our address. I thought there would be the least amount of disruption in our lives if I took care of this during the summer. Big mistake! Although the school administration office was open Monday through Friday, the individuals I needed to deal with were either on vacation, off that day or at meetings. What is the point of being open if you are not going to be available?

The Tacoma School District stated that I would need to go to the Bethel School District where the new address was located in and fill out a Release of Attendance form, which would allow Aaliyah to attend a school out of her home district. The form asked for reasons as to why a release from the school district was necessary and had a place to check if your child receives Special Education. The main reason for our request was that her old school provided daily extensive auditory training, from the audiologist. The new school district did not have an audiologist and therefore, could not provide this service, which was listed on her IEP.

Two days later, I received a copy of the form stating that the release was approved. I was relieved that the approval came through but I did not understand why the form said, "Bethel School District will not be liable for special education costs." I immediately drove to the administration office where I was told that this meant that the school district may approve a release however, they may not release the special education funds that went along with the child. I expressed my concern with this possibility and asked to meet with the Assistant Director of Special Education so I could explain to him why I wanted her to stay at her old school. During our impromptu meeting, I explained that Aaliyah was making progress with her speech, which I believed was due to the hard work of both her and the speech therapist. She had developed a good relationship with the speech therapist so I wanted her to continue to see the same person. Also, a move to a new school would disrupt our childcare arrangements. The Assistant Director nodded and smiled as I talked but I got the feeling that he was not really listening to me.

A few days later, I received a call from the Special Education office. Apparently, the Special Education Director wanted to set up a meeting at the elementary school that Aaliyah would be attending with the Program

Coordinator, the Speech Therapist, the Assistant Director, and me to discuss Aaliyah's placement for the fall of 2002. I thought this meeting would turn things in our favor. Prior to coming to this meeting I filled out the Application for Nonresident admission 2002-2003 for the Tacoma School District, which would either approve or deny her admission to this school district for the 2002-2003 school year. Why shouldn't they accept her, the Bethel School District had already approved her release. I filled out the form and waited for the approval. I wanted to prepare myself for this meeting by gathering as much information as I could covering my rights as a parent and what the school legally can and can't do. I contacted the Washington State's Office of Superintendent of Public Instruction; Special Education Department and they mailed me a copy of the Washington State Regulations.

Once I received and read the information sent to me, I felt empowered to attend the meeting. I came across one regulation in particular that applied to one of the reasons for my request. According to WAC 392-137-140, a district shall release a student if attendance in the nonresident district is more accessible to the parents' place of work or to the location of childcare. I thought this regulation provided a strong support for our request since both my work and Aaliyah's childcare provider were closer to the old school. Another regulation stated that a district shall release a student if there is a special hardship or detrimental condition, which may apply to any circumstance or factor harmfully affecting the student or student's immediate family and is not restricted to a financial, education, safety, or health condition. I felt that if we changed childcare providers this would be an emotional hardship on our family. In order for parents to function successfully at work, we have to know that our children are being well taken care of by people we trust and whom our children enjoy to be with. We were so lucky to have our friend, Cheryl, who was a sign language interpreter and the teacher's assistant in Aaliyah's previous grade watch her after school on the days I worked late, or during school break and summer vacation. She was wonderful and I really can't say enough great things about her. Aaliyah adored her and really enjoyed spending time with her. Aside from us, she was the only other person Aaliyah spent time with since we didn't have any family in the state and I felt we were truly blessed to have such a friend.

After receiving the regulations, I also wanted to speak with someone who knew about school law. There were not very many attorneys in the area that dealt with school law and there were even fewer attorneys that dealt with special education law. After some searching, I did contact one attorney with such experience who advised me of the following three options. One option involved the attorney writing a letter to the school district informing them that the following statement "Bethel School District will not be liable for special education costs" in their Release of Attendance form was potentially an illegal condition. This would be done in the hopes that the district wouldn't want to go into litigation and allow Aaliyah to remain at the school she was attending. The second option would be to go through an appeal process if an adverse decision was rendered. These two options could be lengthy and costly.

The third option was to give our friend, Cheryl, a Special and Limited Power of Attorney with the understanding that Aaliyah would be residing with her four days out of the week. With this Power of Attorney, Cheryl would have the authority to sign, execute and receive any educational document related to and pertaining to Aaliyah's attendance and participation at her old school. Most importantly, this Power of Attorney would allow Aaliyah to continue to attend the school she had been attending for four years. The Power of Attorney would be in effect until we decide to stop it. If we chose to stop it, we could formally initiate paperwork called Revocation of Authority or we could informally have a verbal understanding with Cheryl that things go back to the way they were before the Power of Attorney. The attorney said that he had two clients from other school districts do this and it worked for them.

The day of the meeting finally arrived two weeks before the school year started. I was armed and ready to go or so I thought. As I entered the room where the meeting was held, I felt intimidated because all the individuals present at the meeting sat around a table that was so big it filled the entire room. I am sure that this particular room was chosen just for the purpose of intimidating me so that I would cower to the plans of the school officials.

The Special Education Director began her spiel by saying that one reason for the meeting was to learn a little bit about Aaliyah and her needs. HA! In that same breath she informed me that her job was to make sure that all the children in her Deaf and Hard of Hearing Program were served. If she allowed Aaliyah to continue to attend her old school then it would cost the new district $34,000.00 to do this and this would take money away from the other students. She told me that she would not put such a financial strain on the program and wanted to see what they could do to meet Aaliyah's needs. This really irked me but I wanted to give the other individuals a chance to speak before I said anything. The Program Coordinator jumped into the conversation by saying "You should have no trouble making Aaliyah's 4:00 appointment at Children's Hospital since school ends at 2:40." The Speech Therapist said "I take my three deaf children to the childcare center down the road and they have somebody learning sign language." I had just about had it at this point since it was obvious that this meeting was not to discuss options in releasing Aaliyah to her old district. It was about Aaliyah attending their school and these would be the necessary changes that we would have to make to accommodate the school officials. I informed the individuals at the meeting that my goal was to have Aaliyah attend her old school and there were no other options.

I informed the Special Education Director that her program didn't have an Audiologist, which was specified in the IEP. How convenient that she stated she was working with the Tacoma School District (Aaliyah's old school district) to contract out an Audiologist and if they would provide an Audiologist than the new school could offer this. If they couldn't provide an Audiologist than the Special Education Director of the Bethel School District said that she would release Aaliyah to her old district. I went over the Washington regulation that I had found pertaining to releasing a student if the nonresident school is closer to the parent's work and childcare. The Special Education Director told me that she would release Aaliyah but not the special education funding that went along with her. She would also include a letter explaining my childcare situation in hopes that the old school district would take Aaliyah based on that information. However, I was already told by the Tacoma School District that the Special Education Director would never accept a student without the special education funding.

Well, my last resort was mentioning the Power of Attorney and all eyes got really big and the room went silent. I don't think they were expecting that and of course they said that they would abide by the document. However, they expressed to me that they thought this was an extreme action and would hope that we would not have to come to that. No matter how hard I pled my case, the Special Education Director was not empathetic to my situation. I left with a feeling of unbelief. How could school officials be so callus as to not consider the needs of the child in making such decision? Well, I was determined to keep Aaliyah at the same school but I really didn't know what to do at this point. I cried for a while as I felt despair overcome me. I just finished struggling with Disney about requesting an interpreter and now the school district was giving me a hard time. Call me whinny, but why did I have to struggle with society on some basic issues. Was it too much to ask for Aaliyah to be able to understand what was being said to her during our vacation? Was it too much to ask for the school district to allow her to remain in an educational setting that was more beneficial to her? I just didn't get it.

After I composed myself, I contacted the attorney and informed him that I wanted to go ahead with the Power of Attorney. I called Cheryl to make sure it was O.K. with her. The Power of Attorney was typed and signed by Friday and registration for school was Monday. The attorney told me that Cheryl would need to take the Power of Attorney with her and register Aaliyah for school. She would also need to make it clear that Aaliyah lived with her four days out of the week if asked.

Monday came and I could barely concentrate at work because I was thinking about school registration but since I had not heard from Cheryl I assumed that all went well and I finished my day at work. However, as I pulled in front of her house, she came outside and just shook her head as she held the file I had given her. She explained that she went to the school to register Aaliyah and the program coordinator gave her a hard time. He briefly skimmed over the paperwork and told her that he knew Aaliyah was not living with her and that she couldn't register her.

I quickly called the attorney who stated that the school should not have done what they did and he contacted the school district's attorney who agreed. I was told to have Cheryl go back the next day and inform the district that since it was still summer Aaliyah was not going to live with her until school started. Once again, I went through another day of wondering but when I picked Aaliyah up, Cheryl gave me better news. Aaliyah was finally registered at school. That will teach those money hungry school officials not to mess with the education of my daughter.

The Cheatham Army had won another battle. The sad thing about this situation is that it should nave never been a battle to begin with because a child's educational needs should not be adjusted to meet the financial goals of a school district. Nonetheless, these battles have definitely made me a stronger advocate for my daughter. It is easier for society to ignore the needs of the Deaf because the disability is not seen. Our society is very visual and if a person looks "fine" then the attitude is that there is nothing wrong with that person. Perhaps if a blind eye looked upon deafness then businesses wouldn't be so resistant to provide services such as sign language interpreters. Well, I am here to say that as long as Aaliyah needs me to make sure that she gets the services she needs; I am prepared to get into society's face to make sure this gets done.

What would I like to see happen in the future with Aaliyah's use of her implant? Based on what I have seen, I don't think that it would be unrealistic to expect her to use her implant to the fullest extent after many years of use (oh, say around the age of 18). Ultimately, I would like to see Aaliyah interact with her hearing peers or family members without signing or the use of interpreters while still being able to interact with her deaf friends. I guess I just want her to have the best of both worlds and I want her to know that we chose the cochlear implant route so that these options would be available to her. No matter how Aaliyah chooses to live her life I will support her.

Chapter 11

It's Time for a Change

Aaliyah progressed wonderfully through the first grade and was a few months away from completing second grade when our family received some news that would require a life changing decision. My husband was informed that his office was relocating about 60 miles north of where we lived. This meant that either he would need to commute three hours a day or we would need to move closer to his job. He was willing to commute but I knew this would put a strain on us because we would never see him except on weekends. We discussed our options and decided it was time to move. I tried to make the move sound exciting to Aaliyah by pointing out that she would make many new friends in the new neighborhood and at her new school. However, to date Aaliyah insists that we never talked to her about the move but I remember things differently. Since her best friend had moved away the previous year there were no other kids her age in our old neighborhood. Well, she seemed to take the whole situation in stride and liked the idea of having more friends. I think if she were a teenager the move would have been much harder on her.

Not long after making our decision to move, we had a speech therapy session at Children's Hospital. I told the speech therapist of our decision and she gave me a run down of the school districts that had Deaf and Hard of Hearing Programs as well as a private school for only Deaf and Hard of Hearing children. I heard about this school when we first moved to Washington but it was too far from where we lived so I really didn't consider it as an option. The speech therapist reminded me that if we wanted to avoid the hassles that we experienced with the last school district we needed to look into the different programs carefully and then move to that particular school district. If we were interested in the private school than we didn't want to move to that school district because we would have to pay for the school. On the other hand if we moved to a school district that didn't have a deaf and hard of hearing program, than that school district would pay for Aaliyah to go to the private school.

Based on Aaliyah's progress with the cochlear implant I really respected the opinion of the speech therapist and she recommended that I send her to the private school. She believed it was an excellent school for children with cochlear implants because the teachers focused on daily speech and auditory training in the classroom instead of pulling the children out of the class. Also, the children were expected to use their voice constantly while they signed. I was given the phone number to the school's director and the very next day I called and scheduled an appointment. A few weeks later I toured the school and met with the staff.

At our appointment, we met the school's director, school psychologist, and teacher. They met with Aaliyah and tested her to see where to place her in the school and after that meeting, they met with me to answer questions and talk about the school's philosophy, which included the following: keeping the children on or near grade level academically, teaching the children to communicate in complete English sentences, training the children to make the best use of their residual hearing (the amount of hearing they still have) through auditory training, aiding each child in developing his/her best speech and lip reading skills and developing strong self-esteem in the students through the continuous use of encouragement and praise.

Following the meeting we toured the school to see the classrooms and meet with the teachers and students. This gave me an opportunity to hear the different levels of speech and signing abilities of the children. I was especially impressed with the children who had cochlear implants because they spoke with such clarity considering their level of hearing loss. I liked the fact that all the staff at the school signed so there was no need for interpreters and the school had a small number of students in each class from pre-kindergarten to Junior High. I really fell in love with the program's philosophy and the school itself. After the tour the director said that she would love to have Aaliyah attend the school and I was ready for this to happen. I felt good about the school and felt even better when she said that she liked it. Now, I felt less stressed about the move because I knew where she was going to school even though we still needed to find a place to live.

I made a list of all the cities close to my husband's job that didn't have a Deaf and Hard of Hearing program and started from there. Once I had that list, we then went to the bank to get pre-qualified for a loan while I still was employed so we could get an idea of what price range for a home to focus on. With this information, I went online searching for homes and got an extensive list of homes that I gave to our real estate agent. For the next few months, we spent every weekend looking at homes, which was exhausting but exciting.

Finally, the search paid off when we found our dream home located in Monroe, Washington. The house was 15 minutes from my husband's work and the school district didn't have a Deaf and Hard of Hearing Program. This meant that the school district would pay for Aaliyah to go to the private school, which was 40 minutes away from our house. The neighborhood was full of newer homes and many parks for the children. There was a man made lake, a skateboard park, tennis courts and many trails for biking and walking nearby. Along with the amenities of the city we were set in a valley so mountains and farmlands surrounded us. I couldn't ask for a more beautiful place to live. Everything was perfect because Aaliyah was signed up for school and we had purchased our new home. I continued to work until the end of July and then we were going to move into our new home in August, just before school started. Once settled, the plan was for me to start my job-which I had not found yet-in September. Finding a job took longer than anticipated but I finally started in November. Ironically, I was the one commuting for over an hour each way.

Fall of 2003 had arrived and Aaliyah was going to start the third grade in a new school with new friends. She was very excited about riding the big yellow school bus with other the children but after contacting our school district to arrange for transportation, we found out that she would be the only student on a small white van. The van would pick her up and drop her off at our front door. At first she was a little disappointed but once she became familiar with the driver she was ok with the arrangement. The driver, Julie, became a good family friend and really did make the drive to and from school more enjoyable.

Aaliyah quickly made friends at school and we made friends in our neighborhood. The first day we moved into our house, a few of the neighbors came by to greet us and it was a wonderful welcome. They informed us that there were at least 4-5 families on the block with children Aaliyah's age. I was relieved to hear this and it wasn't long before she made friends with all the kids in the neighborhood. Every time she saw

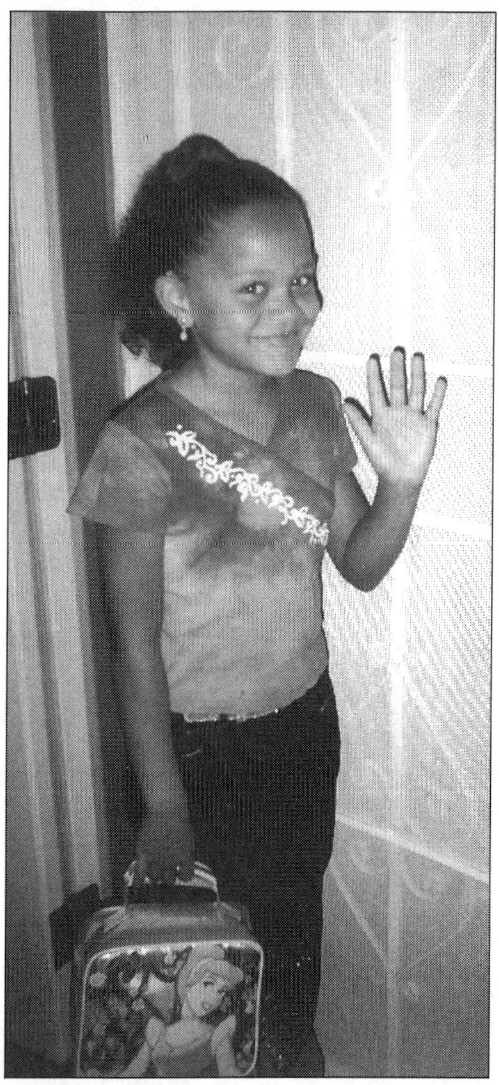

First day of school for Aaliyah, Sept 2003

kids playing outside she would go out there and just start interacting with them. One time I came home from work and saw her writing about herself on the sidewalk with chalk to an older girl. After I got settled, I peeked out the window to see how the interaction was going and apparently they were communicating well, writing back and forth to each other. I was really happy to see that she was so outgoing and not shy like I was at her age.

Getting settled in our home was a lot of work but I had a lot of time since I was unemployed. I think I amazed my husband because in two weeks I had all the boxes unpacked and things put away. Our home was a 2,080 sq. ft. California tri-level, which was a mansion compared to our last home. This was great except it was going to be a challenge setting up assistive devices in the house because of the size. Our previous home was a 1,200 Sq. Ft. rambler and only 600 sq. ft. was living space because of the attached garage. We had a telephone signal light situated at the entrance of the kitchen so the flashing light could be seen from every room in the house unless you had the doors closed. The doorbell signal light was attached to a small lamp in the hallway so when someone rang the doorbell, you could see the flashing lights from every room. At times the lights would startle those who were new in our home but otherwise the lights were great. If we were in the back or front yard and it was somewhat dark outside we knew when the phone rang because we could see the extremely bright flashing lights emanated throughout the whole house. Also, when I vacuumed I knew when there was someone at the door or calling because of the lights. Granted the whole purpose of the signal lights was to adapt our home environment for Aaliyah but it definitely came in handy for us as well.

In our new home we put the telephone signal light in the kitchen and we purchased a door chime with two receivers (strobe lights) for the doorbell. I placed the door chime where the old doorbell was and then I plugged one receiver in an outlet in the kitchen and the other in Aaliyah's bedroom. Now that she is at an age where she likes her privacy and keeps her bedroom door closed, we wanted to respect this by placing a Door beacon on her bedroom door so if someone knocks this causes a bright flashing light to alert her that someone is at the door. All of these alerting devices are portable so we can move them to different areas of the house and they work great.

School was going well and Aaliyah was making the switch to Signing Exact English (SEE) without difficulty. She jumped at the chance to show me the SEE sign for the ASL signs I used and she loved sharing with her classmates the ASL sign for the SEE signs they learned in class. The school's focus on speech was definitely rubbing off because some of her words were becoming more understandable and it just seemed like she was using her voice more than she had before. She was wearing her implant all day until she went to bed and on weekends she was wearing her implant more often but not on a full-time basis yet.

Academically, Aaliyah was doing well. She was a whiz at math and her reading skills were improving. The school mainstreamed the children for PE and computer class at a nearby private elementary school, which was about five minutes away. During these classes, Aaliyah and her friends had a chance to interact with their hearing peers while the teacher interpreted for them. She loved computer class and her athletic abilities shined in PE, which was evident from the fact that the hearing children always wanted to be her partner.

What a ham! Aaliyah poses for the camera

Aaliyah gliding on the ice

The Cheatham family in front of the
Spirit of Washington dinner Train, 2002

Chapter 12

Aaliyah's Growing Up

As Aaliyah grew more confident and independent, I became more and more comfortable with the fact that my deaf daughter was growing up and that things were going to be ok. Aaliyah knew who she was and when an opportunity presented itself, she was right there showing me that she was not going to let communication be a barrier to getting what she wanted. During a school exercise in the fourth grade she was asked to write down how she would describe herself using the letters of her name.

Aaliyah described herself as follows: A is for Artistic, A is for Ambitious, L is for loveable, I is for Independent, Y is for Young, A is for Angelic and H is for Huggable. That is exactly how I would describe her and when Aaliyah was ten years old I wrote her the letter below because I though she might enjoy reading about herself one day.

Dear Aaliyah,

Your Dad and I feel so privileged that God has chosen us to be your parents. We love you very much with all of our heart and want you to know that 110% of our energy goes into being the parents you deserve. You are approaching your tenth birthday with such independence and curiosity. It amazes me how easily you are able to make friends no matter where we go. You are definitely a people magnet because you are so loving and kind. Everyday you shower us with your love and I couldn't imagine a day without your hugs, kisses, and "I Love You." Aaliyah you are a beautiful child inside and out. You have a kind heart and always look out for others, a real mother hen. You always have a beautiful smile on your face and I thank God that I wake up every morning and go to bed every night to that beautiful face and smile. Everyone is always commenting on how they never see you without a smile.

Courage, let's talk about courage. You are not afraid of anything and have gone on adult roller coasters, jet skiing, and yes even a form of bungee jumping all with your dad of course because I am a bit chicken when it comes to this.

Athletic, you are always jumping off of something or doing flips. There have been many times our living room has been converted to a gymnasium. Hopefully, we can preserve some of our furniture now that you actually go to gymnastics in a real gym and we have a trampoline in our backyard (with a safety net of course).

Sensitive should have been your middle name because your feelings get hurt easily. You pucker those lips, stomp your feet and sign "you are rude" as you storm out of the room. Nevertheless, you don't hold a grudge and are able to get over your anger quickly and move on.

Among the above characteristics you are also a very successful negotiator. You are never satisfied with "After the show it is time for bed". No, No, you have to negotiate and sign, "Let's talk for a few minutes before I go to bed." I think I would have a heart attack if you said "O.K." with no questions or negotiation.

Some other information I think you will enjoy reading about yourself is that you are definitely the queen of repetition. You like to repeat a story over, and over, and over, and over. Get my point. Also, an elephant's memory is no match for your memory. If your dad and I tell you our family plans for the day or for the following weekend, you feel that it is your job to remind us oh let's say every five minutes until we have carried out the plan.

There have been certain questions you have asked or statements you have made on a consistent basis. Some of these include the following: Will it be dark soon?" "Will it be daylight soon?" "How far do we have to go?" "Is it going to be a long day or short day at the sitter?" "Do you remember when?" "When can we play?" "Is there more Tom and Jerry coming on? "Never mind." "You are rude." "I need to rest now." "I promise I won't ask you to buy anything." "You can get more money at the bank." "Which pose do you like the best?" "What did they say?" "It doesn't have to be perfect!"

Lastly, over the past ten years we have seen your personality grow and become stronger which will provide you with the strength you need to become successful in life. There were times when you were just a baby that we would worry about how strong you would be to overcome some obvious hurdles a deaf person faces in a hearing world. However, to be honest we think of this less and less and know that that as an adult you will look at these challenges and say "What can I do to meet this challenge versus I can't do this because I am Deaf ?" Right now you want to be an artist, a pediatric nurse or a landscape architect. That's great because you can do any one of these things. Whatever your dream may be, your Dad and I will support you with all of our love.

Love,
Mom and Dad

I will never forget Mother's Day 2004 when Aaliyah was nine years old. She was really excited to bring home a Mother's Day card she made at school but she forgot it. Well, later that day her dad gave her about $9.00 to buy me something so we went to the store. She never bought anything on her own so I wanted to make sure that this was a situation that worked for her. When we walked into the store, I pointed to a candle holder that I thought was really beautiful and made a point of saying how much I would love to have it-after I looked at the price to make sure she could afford it. I told her I had to go to the Customer Service Department but we would come back to the area as soon as I was done. Aaliyah asked if she could walk around nearby while I waited in line. I told her that was fine but not to wander too far. It seemed like I was in line forever but as soon as I was done I saw her walking proudly around the corner with a bag and the biggest smile. I knew she didn't want me to find out what was in the bag so I went along with the act. After we got home, I made myself comfortable in front of the fireplace. As she approached me with a sheepish smile she handed me the bag she brought from the store. I was so overcome with pride that words just can't explain the moment. I asked her how the whole transaction went and she said fine. I wanted more than just fine so she gave me a detailed account of what happened. She went up to a cashier and handed him the gift. The cashier smiled as he talked to her- I am assuming telling her the price of the gift. Aaliyah then pointed to her ear and mouthed the words that she was deaf. The cashier moved the register monitor so she could see the price and then she gave him her money. She said the cashier was very nice and to stop worrying about her so much. Little did she know that one day she would be given that same line by her child.

Aaliyah's flash back to the 60's

There was another time when I was checking out groceries and Aaliyah told me she had to go to the bathroom. Even though we had been to this particular food store chain before, this store was new to us but based on the layouts of the other stores, she thought she could find the bathroom. I asked the clerk where the bathroom was so that if she was not back within a few minutes I knew where to find her. Well, no sooner than I asked, she was back at my side. I asked her if she had any trouble finding the bathroom and she said no. She said that she met a woman and using the universal sign of going to the bathroom (holding herself as she jumped up and down) the woman showed her where to go. I tell you this girl just amazed me.

A few weeks after school started a note was sent home asking the children if they wanted their name entered in a lottery to sign the National Anthem at the Seattle Seahawks football game. Aaliyah, confident in her ability to do this, wanted to enter the drawing because she wanted to be on TV. I told her that it was a great opportunity and to go for it if she really wanted to do it. Her name was picked to sign the National Anthem at the November 21, 2004 game between the Seattle Seahawks and the Miami Dolphins. We practiced and practiced until she knew the song perfectly and when the day came, I was the nervous one. She was so happy and calm about the whole thing. After we arrived at the stadium we were given field passes and my husband had a smile from ear to ear. He was in heaven because what more could a man ask for but to be on a professional football field with a lot of pretty cheerleaders. We brought two cameras to make sure that we had enough film to capture this moment but little did I know that giving my husband one of the cameras was going to create a monster as he took many pictures of the cheerleaders. I told him to save some pictures for our daughter and he replied "It's not everyday I get to be close to cheerleaders." Men! I told him that it was not everyday our daughter signs the National Anthem either. Well, we did get a lot of wonderful pictures on that day and Aaliyah's performance was awesome as she signed The National Anthem. Her hands flowed like feathers but as graceful as her performance was she kept turning her head to see if she was on the big screen TV. What a ham! We were so proud of her and for days afterwards we were still beaming with pride as we showed pictures to our co-workers and emailed pictures to our family.

To date Aaliyah has signed the National Anthem at a Seattle Seahawks game three times and each time is a memorable experience. I am happy to report that my husband has been taking fewer pictures of the cheerleaders. I really don't know what he will do when Aaliyah graduates. He may try to adopt another student just so he can keep this experience alive.

One last example of my baby growing up and I promise to stop bragging. No, really, I will at least for this chapter. In the 6th grade, Aaliyah's entrepreneurial spirit emerged when she wanted to start her own business, a dog walking service. After printing the flyers and passing out the information throughout the neighborhood, we are still patiently waiting for calls, one year later.

Aaliyah getting ready to snorkel in the Bahamas, Aug 2005

Aaliyah performing the National Anthem.

Aaliyah and her dad posing before the game.

It's hard to believe that Aaliyah will be approaching the end of seventh grade. She routinely wakes up at 6:00 am to get ready for school and then gets on the school van by 7:30. She arrives at school anywhere between 8:30 and 9:00 am depending on traffic. Currently she has 3 other students on the van with her but this only started regularly last year. Up until that point, she was the only kid on the van. I have been able to see her off in the mornings before I go to work and then she gets home around 4:30 pm. She starts her homework and then when I get home at 7:00 pm, I help her with the rest of her homework that she didn't understand and correct the work she already did which in essence means that is when my homework begins. While in school Aaliyah continues to use her FM system along with her implant. There was even a brief period in which Aaliyah expressed her interest in getting a second implant primarily because two of her friends received a second implant and really liked it. This was short lived and she remains content with one implant. Who knows what she will decide in the future regarding a second implant.

Christmas Eve 2006, Aaliyah signs the National Anthem

This year has been more challenging because she mainstreamed into her first academic class, Geography. In previous years, she mainstreamed into art class, computer class, and PE. Mainstreaming involves placing a deaf child in a classroom with hearing children, a teacher and a sign language interpreter. You may think that this should be an easy process but it isn't because the student has to learn how to use an interpreter. For example, instead of looking at the teacher, the student looks at the interpreter and if he or she looks away at any point for whatever reason that is information that is missed. The parent, teacher, and student must realize that there are certain places in a classroom that are better than others. For example, you don't want a deaf student sitting in the back of the class and an interpreter in the front because that child can't see the interpreter.

Proud Dad as Aaliyah is on the Big Screen at the football game

Geography was intense for the both of us. Aaliyah had at least 2-3 hours of homework a night but this lessened as she became familiar with the teacher's expectation and her studying skills improved. Although the class was hard and more demanding than any other class, she did well and this gave me a sense of relief. I felt that if she did well in this class then this would be a good indicator of how well she could in mainstreamed high school classes.

Aaliyah has one more year left at her current school and then on to high school. I have started to look into the high school options that are available and have discussed these with Aaliyah. Her input in this decision is important after all this is going to be her place of learning for 4 years and we want to make sure it will be a good fit academically and socially. Currently, there are 4 options we could consider for high school: a local high school with a Deaf and Hard of Hearing Program, a local high school with a small group of deaf students, the neighborhood high school or the state school for the deaf.

The local high school with an established ASL Deaf and Hard of Hearing Program is about 30-40 minutes away. This program has some self-contained classes, counselors specifically for the program, teachers with deaf education experience and some deaf teachers. Aaliyah and I toured this school last year and really liked it. This school had a lot of extracurricular activities to offer the students and they had an ASL class which meant that there would be a pool of hearing students that could talk to Aaliyah. She really liked the idea of coming to this high school with her friends and was excited to have a food court and cafeteria, something she has been without for the past 4 years. I was more concerned about the school's academics. How did the students of this school perform academically compared to other schools in the state? I went to the Office of Superintendent of Public Instruction's (OSPI) Website to look into the performance of each school. This site provided data on how well students did with the state's testing system in areas such as reading, writing, science, and math. It also told me things like teacher to student ratio, graduation rate and drop out rate. This school did better compared to the district and state in the areas mentioned above. The school's website also provided information on the graduating classes ACT scores and SAT scores which were well above the national average. This told me that the curriculum was challenging enough and the students comprehended what they were taught. Well, for the time being I tucked this information in my mental file and office file. On the other hand, some of the other parents felt that this program had problems based on their experience or what they heard from other parents: bad behavior from some of the deaf students was overlooked, some teachers had low expectation of the kids, and students were not encouraged to use their voice or wear their hearing aids or cochlear implants. If a student chose not to wear their device so be it.

The second option is a local high school which is only about 20-30 minutes from where we live. They don't have a Deaf and Hard of Hearing Program per se but there is a small pool of deaf students and the interpreters use Signing Exact English, which is the system that Aaliyah's current school uses. I reviewed their academic performance in comparison to the first high school. Overall their numbers were also above the district and state averages but not as high as the first school's average. There are those parents within our circle who believe that this is the best option for their children because they worked hard to maintain their SEE system and they wanted this to continue throughout high school. They also felt that it would be hard to adjust to ASL perhaps affecting their children academically. I would have to disagree based on my experience with Aaliyah. Initially she came from a strong ASL program and then went into a SEE program. It took her about a month to fully adjust but she really didn't have any problems. I would not base my decision for Aaliyah on the sole factor of a school having SEE interpreters but that's just me. I don't know too much more about this school but Aaliyah and I will be taking a tour either at the end of this school year or in the fall.

A third option for high school would be our neighborhood school. Unfortunately, given the fact that this school is not as strong academically as the first two schools and Aaliyah could potentially be the only deaf student with no support, I would not consider this option. Now don't get me wrong the neighborhood school would probably be a successful environment for the deaf student who has been predominately mainstreamed, has been a strong student and has a mild to moderate hearing loss.

The last option available, although I would not consider for Aaliyah is the state school for the deaf. I could never send her away to school but when she goes to college this may be unavoidable. I have not really researched how good or not so good this school may be because it's not for us. However, some general information I found through the schools website which links to the OSPI site is that the student count was 90. Wow, what a difference from the other 2 high schools that had a student count of 2,000 or more but this student count is similar to the size of Aaliyah's current school. Some alarming information I found was that the graduation rate is 40%, ouch! Granted there may be a number of factors that come into play to reach this statistic but one could reach the conclusion that academically this is not a strong environment. This surprises me because I would think that this type of self contained environment would produce a higher graduation rate, given the fact that everyone signs, teachers and students which means education is being delivered directly from teacher to student versus teacher to interpreter to student. In any case, making the right decision is based on what the family needs and what they can provide. Who am I to judge? What if a family with a deaf child has no other options but the state school because there are no local programs? What if they can't afford to move closer to the school? What options do they have?

Ernest E. Hairston, author of Black and Deaf in America: Are We that Different shared with me his story of being sent to a state school for the deaf and blind. He wrote " I am reminded of my own mother, a young black woman in the early 1940's in the mining town of Stotesbury, West Virginia. Our company-owned house bore the "QUARANTINE" sign when I was stricken with spinal meningitis at the age of five. My mother's only access to medical care was the company-provided itinerant doctor who visited the mining community once a month. Grateful that I was alive and had my mental faculties intact, she steeled herself to make the heart-wrenching decision to send me to the West Virginia School for the Deaf and Blind, but not before exploring the limited number of sources for a cure for my deafness, and going through stages of denial. Later on, after having children of my own, I recognized that it takes a woman of strong faith to let go of her 6-year old boy and entrust him to others for nine months of the year. I realize that my mother understood early on that the only way to compensate for my deafness was to be educated. She wouldn't allow me to use my inability to hear as an excuse to be less than what I could be --an independent and responsible human being."

As parents we want our children to be independent and responsible human beings and high school is certainly a big part of this process but in the meantime, my husband and I continue to do our best in fostering an environment that strengthens our family dynamics and encourages Aaliyah to blossom as an individual.

Along with being an active member of the Student Body Council, Aaliyah keeps busy with extracurricular activities. Wednesdays, after school and Saturdays, after bowling she attends speech therapy for one hour. Now you may think to yourself that doesn't sound like much fun but it really is. You see all of Aaliyah's friends go to the same speech therapist as a result her house is really considered a hang out for them either before or after the speech therapy sessions. Aaliyah loves to go to therapy and gets upset if we have to cancel. The therapist is brilliant because even when the kids are not in their sessions and just hanging out they are still expected to utilize their best speech. I really consider her an angel because the work she does with these children is amazing and her big heart is truly evident by how much the kids and parents including myself love her.

For the past two years, Aaliyah has been bowling in a junior league on Saturday mornings before speech and really loves it. I think she enjoys having a higher average than me and beating her dad at times. I love the fact that I'm a bowling mom and while all those soccer moms are standing outside in the cold and rain, I am sitting in a warm bowling alley drinking a cup of coffee. Another great thing about her involvement in bowling is that word quickly spread amongst her friends and they formed the first deaf team on their league called the Cool Deaf Kids. However, after a while the boys wanted to be on their own team and Aaliyah wanted to be on a team with hearing kids. It's been interesting watching the kids interact with the hearing kids and coaches. For the most part they primarily talk to each other even if they are lanes apart but are very supportive to the hearing kids giving them high fives. In the beginning I was usually the parent that stayed and signed so I would act as the interpreter but now the coaches are really good about demonstrating what they are trying to teach and if the kids need me to interpret they come and get me. Another unexpected benefit of having the kids participate in bowling, other than being dry and warm is that occasionally the deaf bowling leagues bowl after us so this gives the kids an opportunity to interact with deaf adults.

It doesn't matter what the sport or activity, children need to be involved because it builds self-confidence and it's just plain healthy. As parents we need to make this happen. I know from personal experience this may be more challenging with a deaf child because of the communication obstacles and accessibility of interpreters. Throughout the years, except for tee-ball and bowling, Aaliyah has always been the only deaf child in whatever sport she participated in. Amongst her friends, I only know of one or two who have been or are currently involved in sports on a regular basis. Why aren't more parents getting their deaf children involved in sports? If a parent doesn't sign and can't get an interpreter perhaps the thought is why bother if the child can't understand what's going on. Well, I hope parents reconsider this attitude after reading the next paragraph.

About a year ago, I attended an informational night at Aaliyah's school which consisted of a panel of 8 deaf adults who shared their stories about growing up. It was an awesome night of validation because it showed us what our children's lives would be like as deaf adults in this hearing world. There were two important messages in the stories that were shared.

One was to communicate and sign with your children. One of the panelists said that he remembered his childhood as one big "wait a minute" finger in his face. Every time he asked his mom what was said or what was going on, she placed her finger in his face and said "wait a minute". Another panelist said that he didn't like family gatherings during the holidays because he felt alone and excluded since no one knew how to talk to him. He would sneak off to another room and read a book or watch T.V. How heartbreaking is that.

The other message was get your kids involved with sports. One of the female panelist said that she was very involved with sports and it was a great way to meet other people and build her self-confidence. The panelists who were involved in extracurricular activities outside of school were charming, confident and happy. The one panelist who admitted that she was not involved in sports displayed an angry demeanor and barely smiled as she sat with her arms crossed and head down. She shared that while going to school, teachers had low expectations for her and after awhile she just played along.

Along with bowling, Aaliyah is involved in girl's fast pitch softball, which she started last spring. All of her sports have been indoors, thankfully, and so this is her first outdoor sport. I guess it was bound to happen. After she finished gymnastics she really had an interest in softball but I never knew when to sign her up. One day while driving through town I happened to see a banner about Little League tryouts so I jumped on the opportunity. I thought this would be a perfect father-daughter sport and I was right. I didn't have to beg my husband to take her to games or practice he just did it for the most part and Aaliyah loved having him there. This was evident every time she was up to bat and I saw her eyes panning the field trying to find him. Once she did, a big smile just took over her face.

Communicating at the games involved me interpreting and the use of a dry erase board. This was a bit more challenging because I couldn't stand next to her while she was in the outfield. I had to sign whenever she looked my way as I stood by the dugout or during team huddles. However, when she was on the base waiting to score a run, she relied on the coach's signals which we learned ahead of time. If the coach wanted to explain something to Aaliyah specifically regarding a certain play she made then I would interpret to her while she was in the dugout. The dry erase board worked great when I wasn't there because the coach and girls on the team communicated with that.

Aaliyah has always been able to communicate with hearing children without much difficulty usually by writing things down, or communicating in some form of charades. With that said, I know kids can be cruel but I can honestly say that she has not been on the receiving end of any unkindness. However, a few years ago something did happen between a neighborhood child and Aaliyah that actually made me upset. It wasn't anything directed at her but about her, hurtful words that I took to heart. Most of the time I try to take moments like these and turn them into a teaching moment but this time I just get tired and reacted.

It was a really sunny and warm day while the neighborhood kids including Aaliyah were playing outside. After awhile I told her that she had to stop playing because we were going to her eye appointment. Aaliyah wanted me to explain to her friends that we had to go and that she would be coming back with a new pair of glasses. Well, one of the kids said "Oh, now Aaliyah will have three things wrong with her. She can't hear, she can't talk and now she can't see." I was stunned at the insensitivity of this child and angrily replied that there was nothing "wrong" with Aaliyah. This really hurt even though it was coming from a child. At first I wanted to excuse the fact that a child said this but then the more I thought about it I knew that even Aaliyah who was around the same age wouldn't have said such a thing because she just knew better.

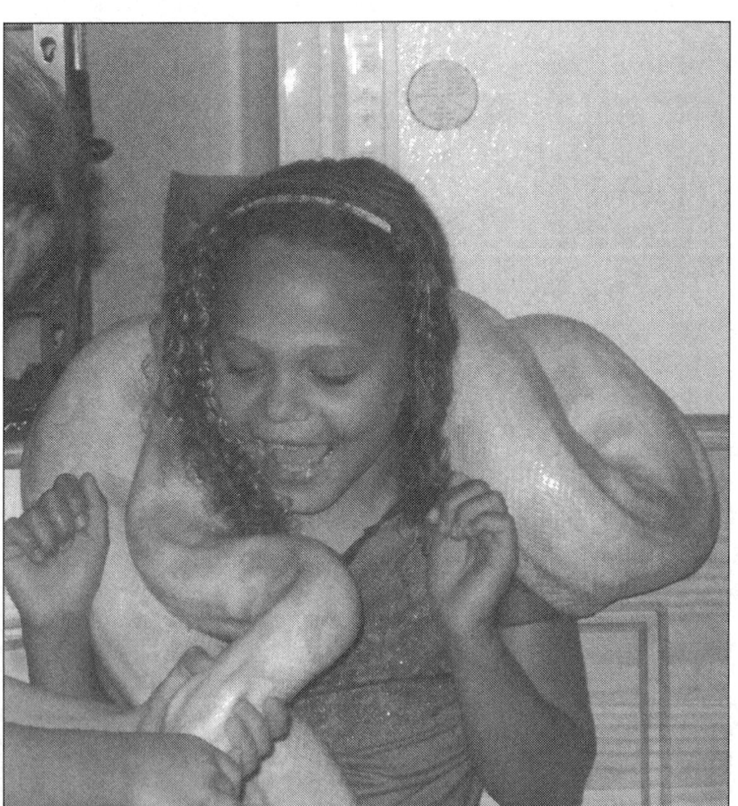

Aaliyah holding an albino boa constrictor at her 9th birthday party with the Reptile Man.

Aaliyah holding a baby crocodile at her birthday party.

I find that the older I get the less tolerant I am of stupid questions from people and of resistance I get from businesses related to the services I request for Aaliyah. For example, one day when my daughter and I were at the mall waiting in line at the build-a-bear store, I struck up a conversation with the woman in line ahead of me. She had asked me if my daughter was deaf since she saw us signing to each other. I replied "yes" and the woman proceeded to grab my arm as if she were comforting me. She said, "I am sorry." I said, "Sorry for what, that I have a healthy, smart, and beautiful daughter whose personality would lighten up any room." I turned to see what Aaliyah was doing and started talking with her hoping to give the woman the message that I was so finished with our conversation.

One day at work I had informed one of my co-workers that I was having a sleep over with some of Aaliyah's friends. She said that I was lucky since it would be a quiet sleep over. Hello! Deaf children are pretty noisy kids because they can't hear themselves talk. My last example of a stupid comment occurred years ago at the park when Aaliyah was playing with some children and a mother and I began talking about our children. She said with an honest look of dismay, "she doesn't look deaf." Trying to hold my composure I told her that there are no physical characteristics with being deaf and I am sure she was shocked to find out that deaf children look exactly the same as hearing children. Sometimes I just have to take a deep breath and say, "Lord, please help these people think before they speak".

My attitude toward businesses has become more aggressive in expecting services and less tolerant to the resistance I am met with. At a doctor's office I worked at I saw interpreters come and go on a daily basis without any problems. It was on file that if a client spoke another language an interpreter would be automatically scheduled for that appointment.

Granted this is a health care setting and not a recreational facility but I think any place that provides services to the Deaf should provide an interpreter no questions asked.

Throughout the years, being a parent has forced me to look at the world with more appreciation and skepticism. I appreciate the relationship that Aaliyah and I have and as she gets older and I get wiser –at least that's what I would like to think-our relationship continues to get stronger. However, I don't always feel like this because my parental insecurities do creep in. I really hate being insecure because it really is a waste of time and it only delays possibilities.

As parents we wonder if we are parenting our children the right way but unfortunately the role of parenting doesn't come with a manual so we are expected to do our best. Sometimes that may not be good enough and I have certainly felt that way when I communicate with Aaliyah. As her vocabulary and signing skills grow there have been times when I just don't understand what she is saying and I can see how frustrated she gets. I have to hold back the tears because it breaks my heart and the only thing I can do at that moment is tell her how much I love her and ask that she be patient and repeat herself. Sometimes it may take a few tries but I usually do get what she is saying. Thank goodness she is so patient with me which I find that most deaf adults are with hearing people. I hope that one day when Aaliyah looks back at her life she can say that we communicated well and had a great relationship. Unfortunately, this wasn't the case for a deaf cousin of mine whom I had met a few years ago. Although our meeting was heartwarming, it was also a bit nerve racking. I have always been a bit self-conscious about my singing skills with deaf adults but she was impressed at how well I signed and suggested that I be an interpreter. This compliment made me feel pretty good about my skills but sad by the fact that here was this woman with her sister, brother and mother around her and none of them signed fluently to her. At our gathering, her family primarily talked amongst themselves while she was on the other side of the room with her own children who signed. During my conversation with her, she mentioned how she wished her family had signed more just like my family.

When Aaliyah was younger a lot of our communication took place while we played together especially on the weekends. She rarely watched TV or took naps so that meant we played games all day so there were times I wished my weekends were "play free". However, now this wish has come true and I do miss those weekends. She has blossomed as a reader and loves to read, especially Manga comic books. She can spend hours reading anywhere from 2-7 books. When she isn't reading, she does spend sometime on the computer and does watch TV. It's really funny to see that some her favorite shows are shows I used to watch like Fresh Prince of Bel Air with Will Smith, or Full House with the Olsen twins and then of course the shows on the Disney channel like Hannah Montana or the Suite Life with Zach and Cody. Sometimes we watch these together and at times I find myself watching the shows without her.

I have always signed with Aaliyah and as her vocabulary grew so did my signing skills. I help her with her homework, talk to her about her dreams, about what's going on in the world today, about what's happening to her body as she develops and discuss issues related to sex and drugs. Any question she has, I'm able to answer because I have made every effort to learn and continue to learn sign language. I am often asked how long it took me to learn sign language. No one can say that they have reached a point of knowing it all in any subject so to say that it took me 13 years to learn sign language would be incorrect. The more accurate response would be I've been learning sign language for 13 years now. When I'm not signing with Aaliyah, I'm the family messenger and interpreter and this can be exhausting. As the messenger of the family my home is full of "Corinne tell Aaliyah to do (something)". In a hearing family you can just ask a child to do something even if they are in the next room but in my family you have to go to where Aaliyah is in order to ask her to do something and sometimes it's just easier to do it myself.

At home as the interpreter of the family, I'm always interpreting conversations between my daughter and husband and constantly responding to "what did he say/she say". Let's face it in a perfect world, my husband wishes he knew more sign language for our daughter but he doesn't and he admits it. For a long time I blamed myself because I didn't make him take sign language classes but you know what he is an adult and I shouldn't have to bug him about learning sign language so he can talk with his daughter, he should just know that he needs to do it. It's been a process but I am learning not to blame myself for the imperfections in our lives and just take responsibility and move on. I think what it really boils down to is that I am getting emotionally lazy the older I get and really don't want to expend all that energy in self blaming. With that said my husband does sign some but primarily communicates in writing or through me. Actually, our set up is quite the norm in a hearing family with deaf children because the mother is predominantly the one who signs to the child and on a rare occasion a family may have both parents that sign fluently.

Although communication is a big part of our family, being technologically savvy is as well. There is so much technology available to the deaf and as parents we need to keep on top of that. The first piece of technology we received for Aaliyah excluding her hearing aids was a TTY. It was so funny the first time I called her because as soon as I would try to end the conversation, she would type something and then reply that her hands were getting really, really, tired. I had to literally tell her that I was saying good-by and it was time to get off of the TTY. I could hear the relay operator chuckling in the background. Aaliyah's big sister called a few times from St. Louis using the TTY and it was wonderful to see her eyes just light up when she got these calls. It was as if the TTY opened up another avenue to independence. On a funnier note though, there have been times that Aaliyah has called family or friends on the TTY only to be hung up on because they were not familiar with it. Well, the TTY at our house is slowly being phased out by the Sidekick 2 (a cell phone with a small keyboard that allows a person to text to another person whose phone has that capability). This piece of technology is just amazing because you can text from phone to phone, send and receive email, send and receive Instant Messaging, and call the relay operator in order to call someone who may not have this technology like grandma and grandpa. This really puts my mind at ease when Aaliyah has a day off from school or comes home from school because we are always in touch.

Granted there are those times that for whatever reason an email or text sent today may not be received until tomorrow. One early afternoon when Aaliyah was home, she had not answered her text from my husband. This concerned my husband because normally she was up by this time so he called our neighbor, a stay-at-home mom, across the street to check in on her. Well, after maneuvering through the alarm system and our barking dog, she made it to Aaliyah's room only to see that she was sound asleep until our neighbor woke her up. The mission was a success and our neighbor reported back to my husband. However, ever since this episode, Aaliyah asked us not to do this because it scared her and she knows to text us when she wakes up. Well, what would you have done in this situation? Just some of the things parents with deaf children have to consider.

As parents we don't expect a lot of kudos for being good parents, however, it is only human nature to feel good when we get them. When I get comments like "Aaliyah is always happy and smiling" or "Aaliyah is doing well in school" I really feel good about the decisions we have made up to this point. It's all worth it to see my child happy, confident, and well adjusted. I certainly don't claim to be an expert on raising a deaf child but I wanted to share my experience of what I have learned and what has worked for us.

One important thing I have learned is that it takes a lot of patience and love to raise a child whether they have special needs or not but let's not assume that these are qualities exhibited by all parents. Let's face it not all people are qualified to be parents and I saw this first hand when I worked in the newborn nursery back in Louisiana. After the babies were delivered it was my job to assess them, give them their shots, and then help the mothers with breast-feeding or bottle-feeding issues. Well, one day a young soldier and his wife had a baby and I asked the husband if his wife was going to breast-feed and if so did she need any assistance. The husband with a straight face said "I am pretty sure that she plans on breast-feeding. When will she get the holes poked for this?" Yes, I kid you not this young man thought that breasts needed to have holes poked before a woman could breast-feed. This was a man who was definitely not ready to be a parent yet. As a nurse, I frequently saw this and it bothered me to see parents who didn't interact with their children in a loving or patient way. Instead, they treated their children as objects that improved their status in society, tax deductions, or a means to collect more assistance from the state. These children usually end up seeing the doctor for behavioral problems or other mental health conditions.

Along with a lot of love and patience, I have found that incorporating the following four components in our lives have been extremely helpful while raising Aaliyah: communicate, advocate, require the best and don't settle for less, and educate (C.A.R.E.).

Communicate: The development of language and communication is important to a child's social, emotional, and cognitive development so it's important to provide access to language as early as possible. Parents need to research the different communication modes and based on the degree of hearing loss decide which mode will be the most appropriate for the family. For example, a child who is hard of hearing or has a mild to moderate loss may do well with an oral approach whereas a deaf child may not if he or she communicates with sign language. Whatever mode is chosen, as an advocate, parents should make sure that every aspect of a child's life from child care provider to school to church to recreational activities is full of language and effective communication.

Advocate: In order for deaf and hard of hearing children to get the services they need, parents need to make sure they are aware of the laws and rights that affect them. The most important of these laws include the Individuals with Disabilities Education Act (IDEA), the Americans with Disabilities Act (ADA), the Rehabilitation Act-Section 504, and the Assistive Technology Act of 1998 (Tech Act). In today's world of computers this information is readily available on the Internet.

Request the best and don't settle for less: The only thing a deaf child (with no other conditions) can't do is hear! Therefore require the best from your child and don't settle for anything less. In other words avoid setting low expectations for your child and make sure you set obtainable goals so that your child's self-esteem can be developed. When utilizing services within the community, require them to provide the best service and don't settle for what may be convenient. If you need to demand for a service that you feel is best for your child then DO SO!

Educate: READ, READ, and READ to your children because it is never too early to start. Some parents may frown upon children watching TV but I think that the closed caption on TV's is another good tool to use to help them learn to read. Remember we don't want our deaf children to graduate from High School with a third or fourth grade reading level. The education of our children should be a team effort between teachers and parents. Parents should educate themselves with what is available to the Deaf related to assistive technology, services, tax deductions, laws, information, etc. We also need to educate the people involved in our child's life who may not be familiar with the needs of the deaf or hard of hearing. Take a moment to educate those who have questions about the Deaf because believe me you will be asked questions so be prepared.

Along with the above components make your house a "Home" by adapting the home environment to provide deaf children with the same environmental stimulation that hearing children receive. For example, hearing children hear the following on a daily basis: a telephone ringing, a doorbell knock or ring, alarm clocks, home security alarms. Hearing children talk with parents, grandparents, and friends on the phone all the time. Shouldn't deaf children have the same opportunity to know that these things are going on in the home? Shouldn't they have the same opportunity to talk to others via a TTY (of course when they are old enough to perform this task)? Also, adapting a deaf child's home is done for safety reasons as well.

Check with an accountant or the IRS to see if any of expenses related to raising a deaf child are tax deductible under medical expenses. Some examples may include: assistive devices, batteries for hearing aids or cochlear implants, sign language materials including classes, out-of-pocket expenses for interpreting services, co-pays for speech therapists and other providers, and mileage or gas driving to and from doctor appointments and schools with programs for the deaf. Also using a childcare provider who signs may be deductible under medical expenses rather than childcare expenses because the provider has a special skill required to care for deaf children.

Having a child who is deaf has been challenging but very rewarding and I would not change a thing about Aaliyah. She is a wonderfully vibrant child who does not let being deaf get in the way of what she wants to do. The ADA on the other hand is something I would like to change. I would definitely like to make this a more clear cut law that would prevent businesses from offering lame excuses such as "providing an interpreter would cost too much money". The ADA needs to clearly state any business that provides a service to deaf children has to provide an interpreter if that child uses sign language as a means of communication. If a program is going to take my money for Aaliyah's participation then they better provide effective communication by having an interpreter present. Issues related to effective communication and interpreters continue to be a major frustration for our family and at times I just want to scream. What good is it to have a law that is left open for interpretation and can't be enforced?

Dealing with attorneys, businesses and the ADA has been a learning process, which will continue as long as we make sure that Aaliyah is treated equally within society. In showing her that we are fighting for her rights it lets her know that we believe that everyone in our family is important which in turn makes our family stronger. I really believe that by incorporating the C.A.R.E. components of communicate, advocate, require the best, and educate, families with deaf children establish a more cohesive relationship. The child doesn't feel like they have to fit in with the family but that the family is learning how to adapt with the child.

Am I a perfect parent? No, but I believe that my husband and I must be doing something right because Aaliyah is a wonderful, confident, emotionally healthy and compassionate person. It really doesn't matter to me that some within the Deaf culture may think it was wrong that we have not immersed ourselves in deaf culture events or that we decided for Aaliyah that she receive a Cochlear Implant. It doesn't matter to me that some within the hearing community feel that we should be more militant when it comes to focusing on a certain sign language system or making Aaliyah wear her implant 24/7 and using her voice 24/7 when she talks. What does matter to me is that my daughter who is deaf continues to develop into an emotionally strong young lady with an infectious personality who loves to embrace life with warmth and acceptance. Recently, she was asked if she had one wish what would it be and she said she wanted everyone in the world to know sign language. Now how amazing is that! She didn't wish that everyone in the world was deaf like her. No, she accepts who she is and the wonderful differences others have to offer. All she wants is to be able to communicate with everyone. What really matters to me is that she be given every opportunity to reach her dreams and realize there is nothing she can't do except HEAR.

Would I want her to be hearing? No, I am so blessed that she is who she is and would not change a thing-really. Parents need to realize that they can't change who their deaf children are. They can't make them hearing by ignoring the fact that they need to communicate with sign language. Effective communication is necessary in order to build a strong family and healthy parent-child relationship. It infuriates me when parents choose to be lazy or I should say neglectful by not learning sign language. They choose sign language as a communication mode for their deaf child by enrolling him/her in a deaf and hard of hearing program at a school which utilizes sign language and they don't follow through with this communication mode at home. This is just heartbreaking and enough is enough.

3 year old Aaliyah and mom at a Christmas party in 1998.

Aaliyah and dad hamming it up in St. Louis, Feb 2005.

Chapter 13

My Life Being Deaf

As parents with deaf children, we have many questions about their future. Will they get a good education? Will they have a lot of friends? Are their friends going to be hearing, deaf, or both? What kind of career will they have? Will it be their dream career? Are they going to marry a deaf person or hearing person? What do they think of our communication choices? Do they think that speech therapy paid off or was a waste of time? The list goes on and on. Let's face it who better to ask how we are doing as parents than our children. With that being said, the value of this book as a tool for parents has been enhanced by the advice and thoughts of the following deaf adults and deaf children including of course, Aaliyah.

The following adults from the Deaf community, Angel, Kathleen, and Favion were kind enough to share a bit of what it was like growing up deaf and what their lives are like now.

My name is Angel and I have been married for 4 and half years to a hearing man. He does sign, but I've taken advantage of my good lip-reading and speaking skills that we don't sign much to each other. I also have a step daughter who is 13 years old and she fingerspells so well that she fingerspells everything to me but includes some signs that she knows. She likes finger spelling so her dad won't be able to understand what she's saying. I hope to have my own kids soon and my goal is to have them be fluent in sign language.

I am almost done with my accounting degree. I graduate at the end of the summer quarter. I worked at Washington Mutual Bank for almost seven years and I got laid off June 6, 2006 and I decided to go back to school to get my accounting degree. After I get my accounting degree I want to look for a job in the payroll industry. I also have my AA degree from 1998.

Q: What was life growing up for you? Was there signing in your house? Were you involved in sports/activities in school? What was expected of you in school by teachers and your parents?

A: My parents and younger brother all signed in the home when I was growing up. They used SEE (Sign Exact English) and a bit of home signs. To this day, my mom still signs, my brother still use home signs. My dad tries to sign but he doesn't really sign. A few of my relatives can sign home signs or fingerspell to communicate with me.

I was involved in several of sports growing up. I played soccer and softball for 20 years (I'm 30 now). Being involved in sports helped me socialize with hearing kids and practice my speech and my social skills. Being involved in sports helped my self esteem build up and I had something to "focus" on and avoid the "bad crowd." I also taught 4 and 5 year olds and 4th and 5th graders beginning skiing and that had a lot of communication. In school I was a captain for soccer, skied, ran cross country, track, basketball and softball. I also was the manager of the wrestling team. I was involved in leadership, yearbook and was on the graduating committee.

My parents and teacher expected me to complete my homework and get decent grades. My parents also expected me to use my very best speech and try my best at everything. I have succeeded.

Q: What are your thoughts about cochlear implants and would you consider getting a cochlear implant?

A: I do believe in cochlear implants. I did not believe in it until my best friend got one two years ago. She barely wore her hearing aids and she has 2 little kids and has usher syndrome. She couldn't hear her two girls' voices and when she got the CI she could hear so much! After seeing her ability to hear with the CI my perspective of CI changed. I do believe if a person has struggled for years to hear out of a hearing aid, they should try the CI. However, for myself, I hear perfectly fine with my hearing aids. I love my hearing aids. It helps me everyday. I do not see myself getting the CI in the near future.

Q: Were you involved with speech therapy? If yes, for how long and did you find it beneficial?

A: I was involved in speech therapy all my life. At Northwest School for the Hearing impaired Children they believed in speaking your very best and I have learned to speak because of the teachers there. They were so helpful and I thank them for that. When I went to my local schools, I had speech therapy once or twice a week. I would leave my last period class for 20 minutes and meet with my therapist. I am grateful for that. To this, day, I have people correct my pronunciations and that is very important to me since I want to be able to speak well and have people understand me. Having speech therapy is beneficial.

Q: What would you like hearing people to know about the Deaf?

A: "Can deaf people drive" is a very popular question among the hearing world. Yes, we can drive, in fact we are better drivers because we don't talk on cell phones, we don't adjust the radios and since we can't hear sirens, we're very attentive!

Some deaf people like myself can "hear" music but can't make out the "words" it's like hearing noise, but we can tell it's music. I always have to explain to people that I can hear music but not the words. I can tell there are words but don't know what the words are.

Q: What advice would you give hearing parents of deaf children?

A: My advice for hearing parents of deaf children is to make sure the child is always involved in conversations! I have been left out so many times in conversations that it made me feel depressed. Face the child all the time when you are talking. Tell people around the child to look at the child while they are talking so the child can try to read lips and understand what they are talking about, or interpret for the child.

Put them in sports!!!! Being involved in sports and activities bring the best out of the child. They meet new hearing friends, build their self confidence and they have fun! You must have signing skills at home and always push the child to do their best. If your child isn't speaking as well as they can, tell them to repeat until they speak clearer.

Kathleen had the following to share: *I am currently in a relationship with my deaf boyfriend and we hope to get married soon. We both attended Northwest School for the Hearing Impaired Children from preschool to 8th grade. We were classmates about three times in the same classroom and we both mainstreamed at King's, a hearing private school, nearby for courses that were not available at our school or courses that were more challenging for us. I graduated from Flagler College with a Bachelor's degree in Sociology. I have been working as a teacher's assistant with deaf and/or special needs students for a couple of years now at different schools. If things work out, I hope to get my teacher's certification and Master's in Deaf Education so I can teach hard of hearing and deaf children. It has always been my passion to assist deaf individuals and a teacher's career is a good way of touching lives.*

Q: What was life growing up for you? Was there signing in your house? Were you involved in sports/activities in school? What was expected of you in school by teachers and your parents?

A: *I was born deaf and the reason is unknown. My parents discovered that I was deaf at about one and a half years old and they were shocked since there were no individuals in my family history that had a hearing loss (not due to old age). The doctor told my parents that like most deaf individuals, I probably would only be able to end up at a third grade reading level. My parents chose to refuse to believe in this fact and they pushed me and made me work harder to catch up with my hearing peers. They decided to learn Signing Exactly English (SEE) instead of American Sign Language (ASL) because they believed that it would be best for me to be able to see the link between English and sing language. My parents made the best choice. Many of my deaf friends have not graduated from college with a Bachelor's degree and this makes me realize how blessed I am with having the skills to be able to do well in school. I was stunned to realize that soon I might be the only one with a Master's degree in my circle of friends.*

My parents first learned SEE then taught me and one method that I enjoyed learning sign language was looking at a big book full of animal pictures or using animal toys and having one of my parents sign the animal name to me. My first "word" in sign language was "light"; for some reason I was fascinated with the table lamp or the room light! My second and third words were "milk" and "dad". My hearing sister was born when I was three and a half years old and she was exposed to sign language since birth. She is very quick to read and understand what I am saying versus my parents because she grew up around me. My parents are able to sing fluently in SEE and my sister understands SEE very well, but her skills are a bit lower than my parent's since she does not always use it.

I did not have a desire for sports, but I grew up taking swimming lessons during the summer and my mom usually was the one who interpreted for my teacher and me. I loved swimming and did well with my lessons. In high school, I joined the volleyball team during my freshman year and used my high school interpreter to go to practice and games. I did not join other sports because I did not have a passion for them. Instead of sports, I loved to read books and create things. That is why people call me a bookworm—I can't read enough books!

NWSFHIC required us to use the total communication method with SEE, which means using our voices and sign language at the same time. After being in a few different Deaf and Hard of Hearing Programs as a teacher assistant or another position, I now look back and realized ho NWSFHIC had higher expectations of their students and made us work harder than other programs did. I do remember many students complaining about how much schoolwork and homework they had, but I do truly believe that because of NWSFHIC's strict procedures, many of us were able to do better than other deaf peers. SEE and total communication may not be for everyone since everyone learns differently, but it worked for me.

Q: What are your thoughts about cochlear implants and would you consider getting a cochlear implant?

A: Cochlear Implant (C.I.) is a hot topic in the deaf community and among parents with deaf and hard of hearing children. I do not have a C.I. nor have the desire to receive one later on. I enjoy being a deaf individual because it is my identity and I find deaf culture to be beautiful and unique. My parents chose to provide me with hearing aids instead of a C.I. because they believed that it should be my decision to obtain one when I became older. I still wear my hearing aids even if I do not understand most of the sounds. It helps me be aware of my surroundings such as the phone ringing or a car going past me on the road. I truly believe that it is the individual's choice to get a C.I. and I am neutral about it since it is his or her decision, not mine.

My feelings about parents giving their children C.I. is awkward and uncertain—it is a big decision and what if it does not work or the child does not want it when he or she becomes older? It will remain in their head and their little hearing destroyed forever. Technology has proved that it can be of assistance to people with a hearing loss through the development of amazing things such as hearing aids or videophones. There may be better options in the future instead of C.I. I did a research paper on C.I. in college and was amazed to discover the statistics. Most studies showed that the surgery to place the C.I. was about 97% successful, but I could not find ONE statistic about how successful it worked. I find it interesting that information regarding the dress of success for a C.I. cannot be easily found.

Q: Were you involved with speech therapy? If yes, for how long and did you find it beneficial?

A: I was in speech therapy from about two to seventeen years old. I tried hard to understand the sounds that come into my ears with the assistance of my hearing aids, but they always remained indistinguishable. The best way to explain how I hear thins is if you turn on the radio or the television to a bad channel without a signal, the sounds are messed up and do not make sense. I do recognize some sounds such as my name or simple words. I usually am able to understand simple phrases better if I am looking directly at the person's lips. I am not the best at lip-reading, but I am able to understand 50 – 60 % of what I say. It is hard for me to decide whether this was a benefit or waste of my time growing up so I cannot really say. I usually tell people that if I were able to speak perfectly, it would still not be successful to me since I am not able to understand what the person is saying to me.

Q: What would you like hearing people to know about the Deaf?

A: I would very much like to have hearing people be educated about the Deaf and their culture. Many schools require their students to learn about different cultures such as African American or Native American. Why not include Deaf Culture since there are millions of people in our country and throughout the world that have a hearing loss? I am amazed at how ignorant people are about how to react or behave around deaf individuals. I will never forget the time when I volunteered to talk about being deaf to the Girl Scouts for my high school community services. One girl asked me if I could cry. I was speechless but recovered by answering that I am normal just like her except I cannot hear well nor talk. I can do just about everything else that a hearing individual can do. That seemed to satisfy her question and curiosity.

Often if I go shopping or to certain places, hearing people are uncomfortable towards me and/or other deaf individuals. Often when I am looking at products, hearing sales associates speak to me unknowingly and when I simply point to my ear and shake my head and mouth "I can't hear," they suddenly become uncomfortable or mumble some reply like "Oh, I'm sorry," before retreating to safety somewhere else. My friends and I have received bad service at restaurants because of our deafness. I have been hung up on the phone, even by my own grandfather once, be using the relay services. Ignorance of deaf individuals' needs can be harmful to both the deaf and the hearing individual. With additional understanding and awareness, more hearing people would be comfortable and prepared as to how to act around deaf individuals. It would make everyone happier. Businesses might even improve in some places!

Q: What advice would you give to hearing parents of deaf children?

A: There is much advice that I could give to hearing parents/guardians of deaf children—but there are some that rise above the others. First of all, always be supportive of your deaf children and show them that you love them no matter what. Show them that you are proud of them; even if their skills may be a bit behind or even if they might not always succeed. If your deaf children see that you believe in their capabilities, this may encourage them to work harder and help them to be more successful in their education. If you show even the littlest emotion about being ashamed or uncomfortable with your deaf children, they will sense it and that will hurt their spirit. With so much against deaf children, they need the most important people to love and support them—their parents/guardians.

It is SO important to learn how to sign in order to communicate with deaf children. If you are able to sign, then the deaf child will be able to have someone at home help with their schoolwork and communicate their needs and thoughts. Even if your deaf children might seem to think your signing skills are funny or embarrassing or not the best, they secretly are happy and pleased that you are able to sign with them. I use ASL as my daily way of communicating with people, but I still use SEE at home with my family or at work if the Deaf/Hard of Hearing Program uses it. I am happy that I have someone to talk to instead of feeling shut out and lonely like other deaf individuals.

It is never too late and you are never too old to learn sign language—even if your deaf children are adults! You can try to get access to books and signing videos and DVD's from the library or bookstore to learn how to sign or improve your skills. There are many courses offered at community colleges or other places. Get your deaf children's grandparents, uncles/aunts, cousins and neighbors involved too—provide them with signing books and/or video and DVD's for their Christmas/Birthday gifts. Your deaf children will appreciate it greatly. My favorite quote from the famous deaf and blind Helen Keller is: "Keep your face to the sunshine and you cannot see the shadow"

Lastly, Favion had this to say about himself, his life, and advice for hearing parents.

I am 27 years old and single. Never been married and no children. I just got a job with Boeing and I will be doing final assembly on the new 787 DreamLiner.

Q: What was it like growing up in your family? Was there signing in your house? Were you involved in sports/activities in school? What was expected of you in school by teachers and parents?

A: I was very much so raised up in a "hearing world" environment. There was no signing until the summer before 8th grade. I was going to a deaf school for 8th grade so I had to take sign language classes during that summer before fall rolled around so that I could communicate with my new fellow classmates. I am definitely into sports and have been all of my life. It has always been a way for me to blend in with the hearing kids on an equal level. As a result, I had a huge desire and motivation to do well in sports so that the hearing kids would like me.

Q: What are your thoughts about Cochlear Implants? Do you have one? If not, would you consider getting a cochlear implant?

A: I do not want to get a Cochlear Implant because my understanding is that is permanent. There are other reasons but that is the biggest reason.

Q: Were you involved in Speech Therapy and for how long? Did you find this beneficial or a waste of time?

A: I was in speech therapy from the time I was about 2 or 3 until I was 19 and a senior in high school. It definitely was worth it. I have had quite a few people not realize I was deaf until they saw my hearing aids. There are not very many people who figure out I am deaf from my speech, so all those years paid off.

Q: What would you like hearing people to know about the Deaf?

A: We (deaf people) are regular people just like hearing people. We have feelings, desires, goals, motivations, beliefs, wants and needs just like everyone else. The biggest thing that I have noticed hearing people doing to me because I am deaf is treating me like I am stupid. Respect that you give strangers that you pass by would be nice towards me also because I am not much different from them.

Q: What advice can you give the hearing parents of deaf children?

A: *My parents never taught me to sign because they wanted to raise me in a "hearing world environment" I am very grateful to them for that decision because 99% of my human interaction today is with the hearing world. I feel comfortable going to McDonalds through the drive through and ordering for myself or buying groceries for myself. I feel more out of place in the deaf community now because I am so rusty on my sign language but I am glad that I have learned to embrace both worlds with open arms and an open mind and an open heart through my experiences.*

Ed and Kathy are hearing parents of 2 eighth grade boys who are deaf with cochlear implants. They wanted to share the following advice with others and parents of newly diagnosed children with a hearing-impairment.

Q: What would you tell parents of newly diagnosed children with a hearing-impairment?

A: Take the time to just breathe, it is ok to step back and focus on breathing, nothing will change in that time frame except that you will be able to understand and deal with what has and is happening. It's ok to cry and let it all out, because once you have gotten it through your system, you can calmly handle anything that is headed your way.

First thing you have to do is get your act together, then give time to your spouse to do the same. Together both of you can move forward with joint strength of the best things you can do for your child and the family. Although your child may have impairment, it is not the end of the world. Dealing with the issues of hearing impairment may take up time and energy, but do not forget your spouse and the rest of the family. If you do, it could develop into a case of resentment. Your child should be on equal footing with the rest of the family in the long run.

Q: What would you like to tell the world about your hearing-impaired children?

A: That they should be treated like normal kids (Maybe all kids should be treated like hearing-impaired children, that way we get through the communication issues that arise), get them involved in activities, do things, be no different than any other family out there. BE A FAMILY!!! So what if you talk/sign at the same time, as long as you are a family, laughing and playing and do stud together, you all will be healthier and happier.

Q: What mode of communication did you chose for your child? When did you get started? Why did you choose that mode?

A: We chose Total Communication, because we wanted our boys to learn to read/write/lip read/talk, as people do. We wanted them to have every option to communicate that we could give them.

We were lucky to find out at birth that our boys were hearing-impaired, so we had a chance to get started early and get them the help that they needed.

We chose Total Communication with SEE. With our technical world, being able to communicate clearly is the key to successfully co-existing in the rest of the world. Reading, writing, typing/computer and talking are the way we advance. We wanted our boys to be able to do all that and have a future in this world.

James and William, Ed and Kathy's sons had the following to say about being deaf.

James: *I think it is cool to be hearing-impaired/deaf because I use my BTE to hear and it is cool for me to read lips without my BTE.*

William: *I am not happy to be hearing-impaired/deaf because I can't hear many things.*

James: *I wish hearing people would understand me and speak slow.*

William: *I wish hearing people would be nice to me.*

James: *I would like to be a scientist, NW Schools' first male teacher, and inventor when I grow up.*

William: *I would like to be a pilot when I grow up.*

Pam, a hearing mother with a seventh grade daughter who is deaf with a cochlear implant offers the following advice: *The piece of advice I would like to give to parents of newly diagnosed children is three-part: Get educated, get involved, and expect success.*

First, get educated. Find out what services are available in your area and what methods of communication are being taught and utilize those services. Pick the method that best suits your child's needs and your families.

Second, get involved. This is everyone in your family from mom and dad to grandma and grandpa! Learn the method that is being taught to your child and learn right along with them. Use this form of communication at all time when you are with your child. Also, don't be afraid to change methods if it is not working for your child. Not all methods will work for all children.

Lastly, Expect success! If you set the bar low, they will meet that expectation every time. But if you set it high, they may not reach it every time, but they will try, and many times they will surpass it. They are very smart children, they just can't hear!

Above all treat your deaf child just like you would any other child, and remember the sky is the limit, don't limit them!

Kaylie, Pam's daughter, had the following to share about being deaf and what her dreams are: *I think it is cool to be deaf because I can always turn off my cochlear implant if I hear a lot of noise. It is hard sometimes to join in with groups of hearing kids because I am deaf. I want to be a Veterinarian when I grow up because I care about animals.*

The last contributor to share her thoughts about being deaf is my daughter, Aaliyah.

I am 12 years old now and can't believe I am in the 7th grade. This year has really gone by fast. Well, this part of the book is my chance to tell the world how I feel about my life and about being deaf. I do like to talk a lot so watch out because one day I might even write an entire book. Have you ever met a deaf person? If you ever have a chance to meet a deaf person do it because we are cool.

I remember when I was little and my mom would tell people that I was deaf; they would say that I didn't look deaf. That's silly because I look like any other kid and being deaf is not what I look like but what's in my heart. I was born to be deaf. Wouldn't that be something if everyone in the whole world was deaf? I know that can't happen but that would be so cool because everyone would use sign language and understand each other. I try so hard to tell people that I am deaf when they talk to me and expect an answer.

I am happy being deaf and I am getting better at understanding people when we communicate. Sometimes though, I get sad and frustrated because people including my own family don't understand me when I try to say something or I don't understand them even though I can lip read sometimes. If you are parents of deaf children and you feel sad that you don't understand them, don't worry because all you need to do is learn sign language. I know that this can be hard and it takes awhile but when you can talk to your child and understand your child you will be happy that you took the time to learn sign language. This is so important for your child, believe me!

I think it is awesome that I can turn my hearing on and off. I love not hearing anything while I am sleeping but I also love to hear the ocean, the sounds of video games and our pinball machine. I can hear all these sounds with the help of my CI-Cochlear Implant. I was thinking about getting a second implant because two of my friends at school got a second implant and they said that they can hear more. My mom told me that I need to wear the one implant I have every day and really, really, get to use to wearing one before I decide if I want another one so we will see.

My parents are cool and I am happy that we can talk to each other. My family makes me smile and no one can separate us!! My mom knows a lot of sign language and we talk all the time. My dad knows some sign language and when we don't understand each other, we write things down. The only other person in my family that knows sign language is my sister and she lives in St. Louis. It would make me so happy if my grandparents, uncles, aunt, and cousins would learn sign language. Oh, well. I have a great life and I love my family because they are great to me but I miss them so much because they live so far away. When I visit them usually my mom, dad, or sister interpret and if they are not there I write things down or I try to teach them some signs so that I can be understood.

I live in Monroe, WA and I love it! The sun really shines a lot here and I love sunshine. We even get to see some beautiful rainbows. One time when we were driving home, we saw a rainbow that looked like it ended close to our house so my mom decided to follow it. We drove about 10 minutes out of our way until it looked like the rainbow had gone into the road near our library. That was awesome. There are so many great things here like parks, a lake, bike paths, and a Fair. I went to my first concert at the fair with my mom and we saw Raven-Symone'. It was exciting to sit so close to the stage and even though I could not hear the music I loved being there because I could feel the music. I clapped and screamed like all the other kids.

I love to play outside especially in the summer. I really like the 4th of July because the night sky is so bright from all the fireworks from around the neighborhood and the fair grounds. When it is really nice outside, my mom and I like to sit outside on our deck and watch the stars at night or the sun going down. We also like to watch the hot air balloons in the sky. My crazy mother said that she wants to go in a hot air balloon one day but I keep telling her no way!

I can't believe that I am only deaf kid in my neighborhood but that's ok with me. I am really lucky and happy to have a lot of friends, hearing friends from my neighborhood and deaf friends from my school. I really love my deaf friends because they are just like me and they make me laugh. They are always there for me. We love to sleep over at each other's home except for my friends that are boys. They are not allowed to sleep over at my house. When we do hang out at my house we are either in the backyard on the trampoline or in the game room playing air hockey, pinball, or basketball.

Besides playing with my friends, I really like school and my favorite subjects are math and science. I think that science is really cool. I love to walk my dog, jump on the trampoline, draw, write and laugh. I love to pull tricks on my parents because we all laugh after it. My favorite color is purple, which is the color of my bedroom. I like purple so much that even Princess' collar is purple. Oh, I forgot to mention that Princess is my dog. Isn't that a sweet name! It just so happens that my name sign comes from the sign for Princess and I have a dog name princess. It was meant to be. I really feel safe with her around because she barks at strangers and when the doorbell rings she lets me know. I taught her how to stand on her back legs when she begs for food. I have so much fun playing with her and I love it when she pulls me on my rollerblades around the block. My favorite TV shows and movies are The Suite Life with Zach and Cody, Hannah Montana, Spiderman and Just My Luck of course all with closed caption. That is when there are words on the TV or the movie screen. My favorite times of the year are summer and Christmas.

I am just like any other kid with dreams, family issues, friends, and yes even a cell phone. Actually it's a sidekick 2 which lets me text or email my parents, friends, and family. My dream is to become an actor because there are not many deaf actors and I like to be in front of people. Recently, I had a chance to be in a local children's TV program that helped people understand what it is like to be deaf. The producer asked me about some of the challenges of being deaf. I told her that the biggest challenge was people not understanding me. She asked me for some helpful tips I could give people when they meet me for the first time? I told her that it's helpful when people speak to me that they not cover their mouth and speak clearly and slowly, but not super slow.

I also want to be a zoo keeper because I like to take care of animals. I know I have to study hard now and go to college but I know I can do it! I am never giving up on my dreams. I think that people should believe in their dreams because that's what's in their heart and life. One of my dreams was to have a dog and I believed hard enough so it happened. I now have a dog! Believing really works!

I want to be successful at whatever I do so I can show other deaf kids that they can do anything just like me. I want hearing people to know that deaf people can be successful at anything. You just have to believe in your dreams and be yourself. This is so important and if you ever have any questions about that just take a good look in the mirror to really see yourself.

Aaliyah and her dog, Princess 2005

Princess and Aaliyah 2006

Aaliyah presenting her school science project 2007

Sisters, Angela and Aaliyah Dec 2005

Horse Riding Camp Summer 2007

Aaliyah Sept 2007

About the Author

Corinne Cheatham grew up in Milwaukee, Wisconsin, with her parents and younger brother. She was awarded an Army ROTC scholarship by the university of Wisconsin-Milwaukee, where she received a Bachelor of Science Degree in Nursing. After graduation she spent four years in the military as a Pediatric Registered Nurse, living in places such as San Antonio, Texas; San Francisco, California; Honolulu, Hawaii; and Ft. Polk, Louisiana. It was at Ft. Polk that she met her wonderful husband Andre and their beautiful daughter Aaliyah was born. The family has since moved to Washington state.

Reference List

1. Allen,T.E. (1994). "Who are the deaf and hard of hearing children leaving high school entering post secondary education?" http://gri.gallaudet.edu/AnnualSurvey/whodeaf.html

2. American Academy of Pediatrics, Committee on Environmental Health. (1997). Noise: Hazard for the Fetus and Newborn. Pediatrics. 100: 724-727.

3. Bellitz, S. "Thoughts of a Deaf Child." The Endeavor. Fall 1995.

4. CDC, Developmental Disabilities Branch. 5 Aug 2004. "Hearing Impairment Among Children." http://www.cdc.gov/ncbddd/dd/ddhi.htm

5. Hairston, E. And Smith, L. "A Poem: The Way of a Hand." Black and Deaf in America. Silver Spring, MD: T.J. Publishers, Inc. 1983.

6. National Center for Hearing Assessment and Management. "Early Hearing Detection and Intervention-Information and Resource Center." July 2001. http://www.infanthearing.org/ehdi.

7. Wilcox, S. "American Sign Language as a Foreign Language." Feb 1999. http://www.cal.org/ericcll/digest/ASL.html.

8. Unknown Author. "Heaven's Special Child." The Endeavor. Summer 1996.

Made in the USA
Lexington, KY
15 November 2018